SOCIOLOGY
SUPER REVIEW®

By the Staff of
Research & Education Association

Additional Material by
Ernest L. Wiggins

Research & Education Association
Visit our website at: www.rea.com

Research & Education Association
61 Ethel Road West
Piscataway, New Jersey 08854
Email: info@rea.com

SOCIOLOGY
SUPER REVIEW®

Published 2018

Copyright © 2014 by Research & Education Association, Inc.
Prior edition copyright © 2000 by Research & Education Association, Inc. All rights reserved. No part of this book may be reproduced in any form without permission of the publisher.

Printed in the United States of America

Library of Congress Control Number 2013932761

ISBN-13: 978-0-7386-1123-5
ISBN-10: 0-7386-1123-9

SUPER REVIEW® and REA® are registered trademarks of Research & Education Association, Inc.

REA's *Sociology Super Review*®

Need help with Sociology? Want a quick review or refresher for class? This is the book for you!

REA's *Sociology Super Review*® gives you everything you need to know!

This *Super Review*® can be used as a supplement to your high school or college textbook, or as a handy guide for anyone who needs a fast review of the subject.

- **Comprehensive, yet concise coverage** – review covers the material that is typically taught in a beginning-level sociology course. Each topic is presented in a clear and easy-to-understand format.

- **Questions and answers for each topic** – let you practice what you've learned and increase your subject knowledge.

- **End-of-chapter quizzes** – gauge your understanding of the important information you need to know, so you'll be ready for any sociology question you encounter on your next quiz or test.

Whether you need a quick refresher on the subject, or are prepping for your next test, we think you'll agree that REA's *Super Review*® provides all you need to know!

Available Super Review® Titles

ARTS/HUMANITIES
Basic Music
Classical Mythology
History of Architecture
History of Greek Art

BUSINESS
Accounting
Macroeconomics
Microeconomics

COMPUTER SCIENCE
C++
Java

HISTORY
Canadian History
European History
United States History

LANGUAGES
English
French
French Verbs
Italian
Japanese for Beginners
Japanese Verbs
Latin
Spanish

MATHEMATICS
Algebra & Trigonometry
Basic Math & Pre-Algebra
Calculus
Geometry
Linear Algebra
Pre-Calculus
Statistics

SCIENCES
Anatomy & Physiology
Biology
Chemistry
Entomology
Geology
Microbiology
Organic Chemistry I & II
Physics

SOCIAL SCIENCES
Psychology I & II
Sociology

WRITING
College & University Writing

About REA

Founded in 1959, Research & Education Association (REA) is dedicated to publishing the finest and most effective educational materials—including study guides and test preps—for students of all ages.

Today, REA's wide-ranging catalog is a leading resource for students, teachers, and other professionals. Visit *www.rea.com* to see a complete listing of all our titles.

Acknowledgments

We would like to thank Pam Weston, Publisher, for setting the quality standards for production integrity and managing the publication to completion; Larry B. Kling, Vice President, Editorial, for his supervision of revisions and overall direction; Kelli Wilkins, Copywriter, for coordinating development of this edition; Claudia Petrilli, Graphic Designer, for typesetting this edition; and Christine Saul, Senior Graphic Designer, for designing our cover.

Contents

CHAPTER 1

Introduction to
Sociology

1.1 Defining Sociology

Sociology is the science, or discipline, that studies societies, social groups, and the relationships between people. The field encompasses both the formation and transformation of particular societies and social groups, including their continuation, dissolution, and demise, as well as the origins, structure, and functioning of social groups.

1.2 The Unit of Study

Sociologists utilize a number of different levels of analysis to understand social life. While some study the social interaction that occurs within groups (the social processes represented by behavior directed toward, affected by, or inspired by others in the group), other sociologists study the social structure of group life. Some are interested in the structure of societies; that is, the organization of populations living in the same area who participate in the same institutions and share a common culture. Others in the field are concerned with the social system, a social group, or with society as a whole unit, distinct from the individuals within it.

Others concern themselves with social relationships; that is, relationships between people that are based upon common meaning, or with social action, defined as meaningful behavior that is oriented toward and influenced by others. No matter what is designated as the unit of study, the focus of the discipline is on social groups and society as a whole, rather than only on the individual, which is the focus of psychology.

1.3 The Perspective: Humanistic or Scientific

Some sociologists adopt a humanistic approach to their work, which means that they see sociology as a means to advance human welfare. They seek self-realization, the full development of a cultivated personality, or improvement of the human social condition.

Alternatively, some sociologists adopt the scientific perspective. They are primarily concerned with acquiring objective empirical knowledge (the actual knowledge derived from experience or observation that can be measured or counted) and not with the uses to which such knowledge is put. They believe that in science one must be concerned with "what is" and not with "what should be." Some sociologists work to integrate both humanistic and scientific perspectives.

1.4 The Sociological Imagination

According to sociologist C. Wright Mills, a certain quality of mind is required if we are to understand ourselves in relation to society. This quality of mind seeks to expand the role of freedom, choice, and conscious decision in history, by means of knowledge. Mills referred to this concept as "the sociological imagination."

The sociological imagination expresses an understanding that personal troubles can and often do reflect broader social issues and problems. It also expresses faith in the capacity of human beings to alter the course of human history. The sociological imagination, therefore, expresses the humanistic aspect of the sociological perspective.

1.5 The Science

As in all other sciences, sociology assumes there is "order" in the universe and that, through methods of science, that order can be understood. The sociologist, however, cannot assume that human beings will always behave in predictable ways. There are times when we do and times when we do not.

Although most of us will think and act tomorrow as we did today, some of us will not. Unlike the rocks and molecules studied by natural scientists, we are capable of changing our minds and our behavior. Unlike the organisms studied by biologists, we are capable of treating each other as whole and complete beings. Hence, the explanations and predictions offered by sociology cannot be so precise as to express universal laws that are applicable to any thing or any event under all circumstances.

1.6 The Social Sciences

The social sciences are concerned with social life. Psychology emphasizes individual behavior and mental processes; economics emphasizes the production, distribution, and consumption of goods and services; political science emphasizes political philosophy and forms of government; and anthropology emphasizes both primitive and modern culture. What then distinguishes sociology from these other social sciences? In sociology the "social," however it is defined, is the immediate concern. Sociology makes a point of broadly considering any and all factors at play when two or more people interact with each other in any context.

1.7 The Theory: Inductive or Deductive

A theory describes and/or explains the relationship between two or more observations. Deductive theory proceeds from general ideas, knowledge, or understanding of the social world from which specific hypotheses are logically deduced and tested. Inductive theory proceeds from concrete observations from which general conclusions are inferred through a process of reasoning.

Deductive Phase

HYPOTHESIS:
generated from theory
and tested through
actual observation

GENERAL
THEORY

ACTUAL
OBSERVATIONS

GENERALIZATION:
initiated from actual
observation and built
on to a general theory

Inductive Phase

Figure 1.1 Deductive and Inductive Logical Thought

1.8 The Theoretical Approach

Sociologists often use the theoretical approach or perspective to guide them in their work. In making certain general assumptions about social life, this perspective provides a point of view toward the study of specific social issues.

The three most recent methods of theoretical approach are interpretative, conflict theory, and structural functionalism.

1.8.1 Interpretative Sociology

Interpretative sociology studies the processes whereby human beings attach meaning to their lives. These processes include the perspectives of symbolic interaction, dramaturgy, and ethnomethodology.

Derived from the work of George Herbert Mead and Herbert Blumer, symbolic interaction is focused on the process of social interaction and on the meanings that are constructed and reconstructed in that process. Human beings are viewed as shaping their actions based upon both the real and anticipated responses of others. Thus, defined by an ongoing process of negotiation, social life is considered to be far from stable.

Actors are thought to be continually engaged in the process of interpreting, defining, and evaluating their own and others' actions, a process that defies explanation in lawlike terms or in terms of sociological theories that proceed deductively. Thus, out of the symbolic interactionist school of thought, the social construction of reality—the familiar notion that human beings shape their world and are shaped by social interaction—was conceived (Berger and Luckman, 1967).

Focusing on the details of everyday life, the dramaturgical approach of Erving Goffman conceives social interaction as a series of episodes or human dramas in which we are more or less aware of playing roles and, thereby, engaging in impression management. We are actors seeking to (1) manipulate our audience, or control the reactions of other people in our immediate presence by presenting a certain image of ourselves; (2) protect or hide our true selves, or who we really are offstage through "onstage," "frontstage," and "backstage" behavior; and (3) amplify the rules of conduct that circumscribe our daily encounters.

In the 1960s, sociologist Harold Garfinkel and others developed ethnomethodology as a system to study the methods used within a culture to accomplish successful social interaction. This approach considers a phenomenon after first studying the cultural values and mores of the ethnic group in which that phenomenon takes place. (Mores are the centrally important beliefs of a group. They embody the fundamental moral views that direct standards of behavior for that group.) This enables sociologists to gain a better contextual understanding of the significance of that phenomenon for that population.

Paradigm	Perspective	View of Society
Functionalist	Macro-level	Focus is on society as a stable system of interrelated parts. Consensus, not conflict, underlies social interaction.
Conflict	Macro-level	Focus is on inequality and whose interests are served. Competition and hostility underlie social interaction.
Symbolic Interaction/ Interpretative	Micro-level	Focus is on process of interaction; individuals communicate through interaction and this communication has symbolic meaning.

Figure 1.2 Methods of Theoretical Approaches

1.8.2 Conflict Theory

The conflict paradigm views society as being characterized by conflict and inequality. It is concerned with questions, such as whose interests are expressed within existing social arrangements and who benefits or suffers from such arrangements.

Sociologists viewing the social world from a conflict perspective question how factors such as race, gender, social class, and age are associated with an unequal distribution of socially valued goods and rewards (i.e., money, education, and power). Generally associated with the work of Coser, Dahrendorf, and Mills, modern conflict theory sees conflict between social groups or within social organizations, and not merely class conflict (Marx), as a fact of life of any society. Conflict may have positive as well as disturbing effects (Coser). Conflict includes disagreement over who gets what, as well as tension, hostility, competition, and controversy within and between social groups over values and purposes.

1.8.3 Functionalism

Inspired by the writings of Emile Durkheim and Herbert Spencer, functionalism (often referred to as structural functionalism) originally took as its logical starting point a society conceived as a social system of interrelated parts and, therefore, analogous to a living organism; each part contributes to the overall stability of the whole. Society, then, is seen as a complex system whose components work with one another.

The components of a society are interdependent, with each one serving a function necessary for the survival of the system as a whole. Sociologists viewing the social world from a structural-functional perspective may identify components of society and explore the functions these structures may perform for the larger system, as well as for its individual members, respective to the importance and magnitude of their contributions.

Problem Solving Examples:

Q Sociology students George and Betty hold different views of wealth distribution in society. George believes that the unequal distribution of wealth is a result of racial and sexual discrimination. Betty, on the other hand, believes that such inequality is a result of society's general practice of offering greater rewards to those with more highly prized talents and abilities. George's beliefs are consistent with conflict theory. Which sociological theory is most consistent with Betty's beliefs and why?

A Betty's beliefs are consistent with functionalist theory. Functionalism holds that the parts, or elements, of society are interdependent. These parts or elements range from the economy to family rituals, with each necessary for the survival of the system as a whole. Thus, sociologists analyze the parts to determine what they contribute to the maintenance of the whole society. For example, sociologists who view the world from a functionalist perspective see the components of society—in the case of the above question, wealth and inequality—as linked and essential for society to continue to operate. Functionalist theorists contend that inequality in the distribution of wealth ensures that the best and the brightest rise to the top.

Q The statement "humans are born fully formed social beings without need for social interaction" is false. How would an interpretative sociologist respond to this statement?

A Human beings are constantly in search of meaning in life—that is, people are always trying to make sense of everyday events. Interpretative sociologists believe social interaction helps humans attach meaning to their lives and they study these interactions to better understand society as a whole. Interpretative sociologists study interactions among family members, factory workers, and in schools. They believe humans shape their actions based on the real and anticipated responses of others. Thus, meaning is constructed and reconstructed over time. This is a never-ending process of negotiation. (See Blumer, *Symbolic Interactionism*, 1969.)

1.9   The Origins of Sociology

It was in 1838 that Auguste Comte coined the term *sociology* from *socius* (the Latin word for "companion, with others") and *logos* (the Greek word for "study of") as a means of demarcating the field, its subject matter (society as distinct from the mere sum of individual actions), and its methods (prudent observation and impartial measurement based on the scientific method of comparison). Comte concluded that every science, beginning with astronomy and ending with sociology, follows the same regular pattern of development.

The first stage in this development is the theological stage. In the theological stage, scientists look toward the supernatural realm of ideas for an explanation of what they observed. In the second, or metaphysical stage, scientists begin to look to the real world for an explanation of what they have observed.

Finally, in the positive stage, which is defined as the definitive stage of all knowledge, scientists search for general ideas or laws. With knowledge of society, such as how society is held together (social statics) and how society changes (social dynamics) people can predict and, thereby, control their destiny. They can build a better and brighter future for themselves.

Was Comte's conception of a science of society ahead of its time, or was his conception of a science that would allow human beings control over their lives timely? If one only considers the fast pace of technological and social change in Europe during the eighteenth century, the proliferation of factories, the spread of cities and of city life, and the loss of faith in "rule by divine right," then it would be timely. However, if one considers intellectual history, notwithstanding the accomplishments of Harriet Martineau, who was observing English social patterns at the same time that Comte was laying a foundation for sociology; Karl Marx, "the theoretical giant of communist thought" whose prophecies are still being hotly debated; and Herbert Spencer, whose idea was that society follows a natural evolutionary progression toward something better, then Comte was clearly ahead of his time. More than 50 years passed before Emile Durkheim, in his statistical study of suicide, and Max Weber, in a series of studies in which he sought to explain the origins of capitalism, came along and tested Comte's ideas.

In the beginning of the twentieth century, under the influence of Lester Ward and William Graham Sumner, American sociology experienced a loss of interest in the larger problems of social order and social change and began to concentrate on narrower and more specific social problems. Until 1940, attention in the discipline was focused at the University of Chicago, where George Herbert Mead was originating the field of social psychology. Robert Park and Ernest Burgess were concentrating on the city and on such social problems as crime, drug addiction, prostitution, and juvenile delinquency.

By the 1940s, attention began to shift away from reforming society toward developing abstract theories of how society works and standardizing the research methods that sociologists employ. Talcott Parsons, the famed functionalist, touched a generation of sociologists by advocating grand theory—the building of a theory of society based on aspects of the real world and the organization of these concepts to form a conception of society as a stable system of interrelated parts.

Robert Merton proposed building middle-range theories from a limited number of assumptions from which hypotheses are derived. Merton also distinguished between manifest, or intended, and latent, or unintended, consequences of existing elements of social structure which are either functional or dysfunctional to the system's relative stability. This movement succeeded despite the efforts of C. Wright Mills to reverse the trend away from activism, as well as Dennis Wrong's attempt to end the "oversocialized," or too socially determined, conception of "man in sociology."

No single viewpoint or concern has dominated the thinking of sociologists since the 1970s. The question of whether a sociologist can or should be detached and value-free, and the question of how a sociologist deals with the individual, remain controversial. Thus, sociologists have yet to agree on whether the goals of sociology are description, explanation, prediction, or control. More recently, sociologists have begun to use sociological knowledge with the intent of applying it to human behavior and organizations. Such knowledge can be used to resolve current social problems. For example, while some sociologists may study race relations and patterns of contact between minority and majority groups, applied sociologists may actually devise and implement strategies to improve race relations in the United States.

1.10 Careers in Sociology

Sociologists often teach at the college or university level. Some combine teaching and research. Others work full time as researchers. As researchers, sociologists may work in a variety of settings: private industry, government, schools and school boards, research foundations, voluntary organizations, or on their own as consultants or grant recipients. They may be studying issues related to population, health, advertising, crime, government, science, the environment, architecture, cities, and urban life. For instance, they may be writing, analyzing, and administering surveys; analyzing census data; or evaluating programs.

For students contemplating careers in social research, criminology, demography, immigration, social psychology, public administration, government, gerontology, the military, and market research, sociology can be a valuable liberal arts major. For those planning careers in law, medicine, community planning, architecture, and politics, sociology offers valuable insights and critical skills.

Quiz: Introduction to Sociology

1. Sociology is best defined as the scientific study of

    (A)   social problems.

    (B)   human personality.

    (C)   social interaction.

    (D)   human development.

    (E)   attitudes and values.

2. Sociology first developed as a distinct discipline in the _____ century.

    (A) sixteenth

    (B) seventeenth

    (C) eighteenth

    (D) nineteenth

    (E) twentieth

3. Which of the following concepts is most clearly at the core of the sociological theory known as functionalism?

    (A) Economic development

    (B) Class conflict

    (C) Human communication

    (D) Intellectual creativity

    (E) Interdependence

4. At its most encompassing level, the "sociological imagination" links individual experience to

    (A) psychological predispositions.

    (B) family background.

    (C) forces in the larger society.

    (D) racial identity.

    (E) population patterns.

5. Concepts such as exploitation, inequality, and power relationships are most clearly associated with which sociological theory?

    (A) Functionalist

    (B) Conflict

    (C) Interactionist

    (D) Evolutionary

    (E) Dramaturgical

6.   The coining of the term *sociology* from the Latin word *socius* and the Greek term *logos* formulated a new concept introduced by

    (A) Comte.

    (B) Moreno.

    (C) Freud.

    (D) Weber.

    (E) O'Neill.

7.   The sociological perspective that tends to look at social institutions as creating and maintaining an unequal division between the haves and the have-nots and as constantly characterized by struggles for power best describes

    (A) the functionalist perspective.

    (B) the conflict perspective.

    (C) the symbolic interactionist perspective.

    (D) the interpretative perspective.

    (E) None of the above.

8.   Sociologists are said to take an inductive approach when they move from _____ to hypothesis.

    (A) speculation

    (B) experimentation

    (C) theory

    (D) observations

    (E) None of the above.

9. Those sociologists who study group interactions to acquire objective knowledge, without consideration for the uses to which such knowledge will be put, are often described as

   (A) Marxist.

   (B) interpretative.

   (C) humanistic.

   (D) conflict theorists.

   (E) scientific.

10. Interpretative sociology is concerned with the meanings human beings attach to their lives. This perspective was derived from the work of

   (A) Blau and Duncan.

   (B) Mead and Blumer.

   (C) Freud and Piaget.

   (D) Durkheim and Piaget.

   (E) Marx and Weber.

ANSWER KEY

1.	(C)	6.	(A)
2.	(D)	7.	(B)
3.	(E)	8.	(D)
4.	(C)	9.	(E)
5.	(B)	10.	(B)

CHAPTER 2

The Methods of Research

2.1 Defining Research Methods

The term *research methods* refers both to a strategy or plan for carrying out research and the means of carrying out the strategy. Some sociologists favor quantitative methods. Following the example of the natural sciences, they make use of statistical and other mathematical techniques of quantification or measurement in their efforts to describe and interpret their observations. Others favor qualitative methods, relying on personal observation and description of social life in order to explain behavior. Conceding that their methods entail the loss of precision, they argue that their methods achieve a deeper grasp of the texture of social life. Thus, Max Weber developed the method of *Verstehen*.

Verstehen is understanding as a means of characterizing and interpreting or explaining. This is done by applying reason to the external and internal context of specific social situations, such as the origins of Western capitalism. Max Weber used the method of Verstehen to justify the thesis of his book *The Protestant Ethic and the Spirit of Capitalism*. In it, he analyzes the forces at work in the swift and solid economic success of the United States in (at the time) only 100 years of history. He pointed out that a combination of seemingly unlimited natural resources and a religious ethic based on delaying or forgoing any gratification promoted a dogmatic and steady growth in American wealth.

2.2 Survey Research

Sociologists most often use the survey method of observation in their research. Subjects are asked about their opinions, beliefs, or behavior, such as how they have behaved in the past or how they intend to behave in the future, in a series of questions. The information is collected from the respondents of the survey directly by means of an interview, or indirectly by means of a self-administered written form of a questionnaire that the respondents fill out themselves. Interviews may be conducted in person, by phone, or by some other electronic means of communication, such as e-mail.

The interview may be structured, or close-ended, where respondents are asked a series of questions in which they are given a limited choice between several possible responses on each question. The interview may also be unstructured, or open-ended, where respondents are asked questions to which they can respond freely in their own words. The use of a combination of both open-ended and close-ended questions may also be utilized. The researcher may be interested in determining or gauging the general characteristics of a population or in collecting information about some event from the persons involved.

Surveys can be mainly descriptive, exploratory, or explanatory, each with its own purpose. A descriptive survey answers the "what" questions in that it gives an account, in full detail, of what is present in a given situation, group, or event. An exploratory survey answers "how" questions by describing what is going on, and how things occur, such as how people interact with each other. Lastly, explanatory surveys focus on discovering or understanding either causal or correlational relationships between variables. Variables are characteristics or attributes relevant to the object of study that can be classified as either dependent or independent. A *dependent* variable is one that is affected by another variable. For example, the *dependent* variable of political attitude is influenced by the *independent* variables of age, gender, and race. These pairs, therefore, create cause-and-effect relationships. A control is a technique for differentiating between outside factors that may or may not influence the relationships between variables. Such relationships between two variables can be either correlational or causal. When variables are correlational, a change in one coincides with, but does not necessarily cause, a change in the other. A causal relationship exists between variables when a change in one variable directly triggers or forces a change in the other.

How, then, is survey research carried out? First, a population is selected. In the case of a relatively small population, all members can be approached and surveyed separately, as is true in the case of an event that requires collecting information from certain key persons involved. If the population is relatively large, a sample will be selected for study from the entire population. A representative sample is one that accurately reflects the population from which it is drawn. A random sample is one where every member of the population has the same chance of being chosen for study, as could be selected by throwing the names of everyone in a hat, mixing them up, and selecting as many as are thought necessary to obtain representatives. Systematic sampling is a type of sample in which each nth unit in a list is selected for inclusion in the sample. For example, every fiftieth resident listed in a phone book of a given area will be selected. In this way, every member of the population is guaranteed the same chance of being selected for study.

Stratified sampling uses the differences that already exist in a population, such as between males and females, as the basis for selecting a sample. Knowing the percentage of the population that falls into a particular category, the researcher then randomly selects a number of persons to be studied from each category in the same proportion as exists in the population.

2.3 Experimentation

Sociologists can and sometimes do conduct experiments. In the broadest sense, experimentation involves the observation, measurement, and calculation of the consequences of an action. Typically, the social science researcher selects a group of subjects to be studied (the experimental group), exposes them to a particular condition, and then measures the results. The researcher usually measures the results against that of a control group (a similar population upon which the action has not been performed). Experiments are used to test theories and the hypotheses drawn from them. In one type of experiment, researchers create a situation in which they test the extent of the relationship that presumably exists between an independent and a dependent variable, by means of introducing a third variable.

Experiments may be carried out in a laboratory or in the field. Field experiments are carried out in natural settings. In one of the most famous field experiments of social science, conducted in the 1930s, Elton May identified what has come to be known as the Hawthorne effect—the fact that the mere presence of a researcher affects the subject's behavior.

2.4 Observation

Observation is a technique that provides firsthand experience of real situations. Unobtrusive observation is observation from a distance, without being involved in the group or activity being studied. Unobtrusive observation may be observing subjects from afar (e.g., watching children play in a schoolyard) or observing subjects more closely (e.g., watching children play in a classroom from behind a one-way mirror).

Often referred to as field research, participant observation is observation by a researcher who is (or appears to be) a member of the group or a participant in the activity he/she is studying. Participant observers may or may not conceal their identities as researchers. They may conceal their identities as researchers so as not to influence their subjects who, not knowing they are being observed, will act naturally. On the other hand, they may disclose their identities as researchers and seek to minimize their influence by not allowing themselves to get too involved with subjects while they are establishing a rapport.

2.5 Secondary Analysis

Secondary analysis refers to the analysis of existing sources of information. In the hope of discovering something new, the researcher examines old records and documents, including archives and official statistics provided by the government, e.g., a national census bureau. Thus, by using available data, the researcher avoids having to gather information from scratch. By analyzing old records and documents, the researcher can acquire an understanding of relations between people in the past.

Content analysis refers to the techniques employed to describe what is contained within the documentation. The contents may be quantitative, citing mathematically derived data such as percentages, rates, or averages to describe, for example, various societal conditions or types of human activity by way of arithmetic means, modes, or medians. Information may also be qualitative, using concepts together with reason to capture observations for analysis.

Problem Solving Example:

Q Roger would like to study preschool children in a public housing community to determine whether patterns of social interaction between these children differ significantly from those of children living in a middle-class suburb. Roger has applied to work in a day-care center run by the public housing authority in his area. He will keep extensive notes on the interactions of the children—whom they befriend, how they play with one another, how they interact with adult supervisors, and so on. He will do the same at the private middle-class day-care center outside the city. Describe the method of research Roger has chosen. Why is this preferable for this study?

A Roger has chosen participant observation or field research. In field research, the social scientist becomes a member of the group being studied, either with or without informing the subjects of his intention. (In the above scenario, Roger will be one of the children's supervisors.) Some field researchers conceal their identities so as not to influence the behavior of their subjects. Others disclose their identities,

Method	Use	Advantages	Disadvantages
Survey	Not directly observable information; can be gathered through the use of a survey; for example, attitudes and values	Generates information on large numbers of people; can provide in-depth information as well	Low return rate of surveys can create "selections" effect
Experimentation	Experimentation is used when trying to ascertain the specific relationship among variables; for example, a causal relationship	Allows cause-effect relationship to be established; research is more easily replicated in this highly controlled environment	Difficult to generalize results due to the oftentimes extremely artificial setting of a laboratory; may bias individuals' behavior
Observation	Observation is used to explore behavior in "natural" settings; directly observable behavior	Allows "natural" behavior to be observed	Difficult to replicate; more prone to researcher bias; can be time-consuming
Secondary Analysis	Secondary analysis is used for either exploratory or explanatory research	Allows historical materials to be used; can be less costly using already-existing data	No ability for the researcher to add or alter data

Figure 2.1 Review of Four Methods of Research

but distance themselves from the subjects' activities in an effort to lessen their own influence on the subjects' behavior.

In this situation, field research is preferable to other research methods, such as survey, experimentation, and/or secondary analysis. Roger might interview the preschoolers as part of field research to gain insights into specific behaviors, but observation will give him a more objective view of their social patterns as a whole. Likewise, if Roger had chosen laboratory experimentation as his method, the experiment might show how the children interact in specific, controlled conditions but would not show patterns of interaction in a natural environment. Secondary analysis would most likely not be helpful, since it is unlikely that records detailing this type of subject exist.

2.6   The Stages of Research

Research is a process that includes:

1. Defining the problem or determining the unit of study—the questions, issues, or topics with which one is concerned.

2. Identifying and reviewing the relevant literature bearing upon the problem.

3. Formulating a hypothesis—a tentative statement about what one expects to observe, e.g., the prediction of a relationship between variables, or the prediction that a certain relation between people will be obtained.

4. Selecting and implementing a research design to test one's hypothesis—the plan for collecting and analyzing information.

5. Drawing a conclusion—determining whether or not one's hypothesis is confirmed, and presenting one's findings in an organized way that both describes and, wherever possible, explains what one has observed.

2.7   Ethical Problems

Sociologists can and often do encounter ethical problems or dilemmas in conducting research. Some of the following are concerns of sociologists who perform this research:

1. What harm, if any, is the research likely to bring to participants? Does the knowledge gained justify the risks involved?

2. Is the privacy of subjects being invaded, and should the privacy of subjects be maintained under all circumstances?

3. Do subjects have a right to be informed that they are being studied? Is their consent necessary?

4. Does it matter how the research results will or can be applied? Should this affect the research design or the way in which the research is reported?

5. When, if at all, is deception in conducting research or in reporting the research results justified?

Problem Solving Example:

Q   Mary and Peter are conducting research on the money-saving habits of college students. They are conducting comprehensive face-to-face interviews with their subjects, but have buried their questions about personal savings among questions about behaviors like eating, sleeping, and study habits. They believe that concealing the questions in this manner will improve their chances of getting candid responses. With that in mind, they have intentionally misled the subjects by telling them that the objective of the study is to determine the effect of academic stress on relationships among college students. What ethical consideration(s) are contained in Mary and Peter's research?

A   Sociologists must weigh the benefits of the research against the possible harm that might result from it. In sociological research, this "harm" is not usually physical harm, but the kind of harm that comes from concealing the true intent of the research from subjects. The questions asked may influence the subjects to behave in certain ways based on their perceptions of what the researcher is alluding to in his work. This could corrupt the data. Also, subjects may develop certain expectations based on what they believe to be the purpose of the study. Their decision to participate in the study may be based on that implied purpose. When the subjects discover that the information was used for some other purpose (one which they may not believe to be as noble or significant), they may become disillusioned and be discouraged from participating in future information gathering studies of any kind.

Quiz: The Methods of Research

1. A general difficulty encountered in doing social research is that

    I.   ethical considerations prevent certain types of research from taking place.

    II. it deals with subjects who are self-aware and whose behavior is not always predictable.

    III. social researchers are part of the phenomenon they study.

    IV. the methods of social research are more advanced than those of other disciplines.

    (A) II only.

    (B) III only.

    (C) IV only.

    (D) I and III only.

    (E) I, II, and III only.

2. The research method that involves a social scientist living among and interacting with the people being studied is known as

    (A) survey research.

    (B) experimentation.

(C)   content analysis.

(D)   participant observation.

(E)   strategic engagement.

3.   The research method that relies on interviews with a randomly selected sample of people is known as

(A)   survey research.

(B)   participant observation.

(C)   content analysis.

(D)   experimentation.

(E)   exploratory research.

4.   A researcher studying the diaries of Holocaust victims would be using which method to carry out research?

(A)   Survey

(B)   Participant observation

(C)   Obtrusive research

(D)   Content analysis

(E)   none of the above

5.   In order to get a sample of Los Angeles residents for a survey on political attitudes, Carmen selects every 1000th person from the Los Angeles city phone book. This is an example of _____ sampling.

(A)   random

(B)   systematic

(C)   cluster

(D)   stratified

(E)   non-representative

6. "Female college athletes will have higher academic averages than male college athletes." In this hypothesis, which is the independent variable?

    (A) Athletic participation

    (B) College attendance

    (C) Academic achievement

    (D) Gender

    (E) Study habits

7. Often in conducting scientific research, social scientists must determine whether the knowledge to be gained justifies the _____ involved.

    (A) risks

    (B) financial costs

    (C) time

    (D) concepts

    (E) principles

8. The application of reason to the external and internal context of social situations was developed by the early sociologist Max Weber. This method is called

    (A) Verstehen.

    (B) Gesellschaft.

    (C) Gemeinschaft.

    (D) theory.

    (E) experimentation.

9.   A crucial part of research is the formulation of a tentative state-
     ment about what one expects to observe. This statement is called
     the

     (A) theory.

     (B) hypothesis.

     (C) diagnosis.

     (D) principle.

     (E) All of the above.

10. In experimentation, sociologists often use two similar groups, one
     of which does not undergo the action applied to the other. The
     latter group is called the experimental group. The first group is
     called the _____ group.

     (A) proxy

     (B) beta

     (C) control

     (D) alpha

     (E) None of the above.

ANSWER KEY

1.	(E)	6.	(D)
2.	(D)	7.	(A)
3.	(A)	8.	(A)
4.	(D)	9.	(B)
5.	(B)	10.	(C)

CHAPTER 3

Socialization

3.1 The Process of Socialization and Self-Formation

Socialization is the process through which we learn or are trained to be members of society, to take part in new social situations, or to participate in social groupings. In other words, it is the prescriptive term in sociology for the process of being "social."

Generally, sociologists consider the process of socialization to be based on social interaction, the ways in which we behave toward and respond to one another; however, not all sociologists agree on what is formed by such interactions. Does interaction imply that society, social groups, social structure, or human beings make the perpetuation and transformation of a particular culture possible? Sociologists tend to differ in their opinions of what is learned, produced, reproduced, or altered in the process of socialization: (1) in their orientation toward society, social groups, social structure, or man-made culture; and (2) in their conception of the part, if any, human biology and individual psychology play in socialization.

3.1.1 Primary and Secondary Forms of Socialization

Sociologists hold the view that the individual cannot develop in the absence of the social environment—the groups within which interaction takes place and socialization occurs. Within this context, primary socialization refers to the initial socialization that a child receives through which he or she becomes a member of society (i.e., learning and coming to share the social heritage or culture of a society through the groups into which he or she is born). Secondary socialization refers to the subsequent experience, of socialization into new sectors of society by an already socialized person.

3.1.2 Personality

Socialization is the process through which personality is acquired and is reflective of the society in which that process occurs. An individual's socialization is marked by the fairly consistent patterns shown in the thoughts, feelings, and activities representative of the individual. Socialization is the essential link between the individual and the surrounding social realms, without which neither is thought to be capable of surviving.

Socialization not only makes it possible for society to perpetuate itself (keep itself in existence beyond the current generation into the future), but also allows individuals within the same generation to relate to each other in the form of culture, heritage, and the social circumstances generated when going through life's course of birth, childhood, maturity, old age, and death.

Assuming that the content of socialization varies from one person to the next as a consequence of the influence of various cultures and subcultures, including race, class, region, religion, and groups in society, then every person should be different. Most of the differences would be a product of socialization, with the remainder being the result of the random impact of relatively different social and cultural environments.

The socialization process is thought to explain both the similarities in personality and social behavior of the members of society and the differences that exist in society between one person and the next. The view of most social scientists is that it does not matter that the two factors of nature and nurture are intimately related and cannot be separated. Hence, the part that human biology plays in socialization (i.e., of nature in nurture) cannot be accurately measured. Heredity represents a basic potential, the outlines and limits of which are biologically fixed, because the socialization process is thought to be all-important to the development of personality.

Consistent with a view held by modern psychologists, it is argued that any instincts (unlearned, inherited behavior patterns that human beings once had) have been lost in the course of human evolution. There is no human nature outside of what culture makes of us. Hence, there is the concern that children raised in isolation or in institutions, who have little or no opportunity to develop the sorts of emotional ties with adults that make socialization possible, will be devoid of personality and will lack the social skills necessary to face even the simplest of life's challenges.

The process of becoming human in the sense of being able to participate in society is understood to be the process of socialization. The self at the core of personality, the individual's conscious experience of having a separate unique identity, is thought to be a social product objectively created and transformed throughout a person's life by interaction with others.

3.2   Agents of Socialization

The various agents of socialization are the individuals, groups, and institutions that supply the structure through which socialization takes place in modern societies.

3.2.1   The Family

Generally considered the most basic social institution, the family is a union that is sanctioned by the state and often by a religious institution, such as a church. As such, the family provides continuity in areas such as language, personality traits, religion, and class. The family is generally believed to be the most important agent of socialization in a child's social world until schooling begins. Although the school and peer group become central to social experience as the child grows older, the family remains central throughout the entire life course.

3.2.2   School

As the social unit devoted to providing an education, the school provides continuity both in cognitive skills and in the indoctrination of values. Many subject areas of knowledge that may or may not be available at home, or that the modern home is ill-equipped to provide, are also provided by the school. Unlike the family, which is based on personal relationships, the child's social experiences in school broaden to include people of a variety of social backgrounds. It is there that children learn the importance society gives to race, gender, and class.

3.2.3 Peer Groups

As a primary group whose members are roughly equal in status, peer groups (such as play groups) provide continuity in lifestyles. Although first peer groups generally consist of a young child's neighborhood playmates, as the child meets new people at school and becomes involved in other activities, the peer group expands. It is in the peer group where the child, free of direct supervision from adults, comes to define him- or herself as independent from the family. During adolescence, the peer group becomes particularly important to the child and sometimes proves to be a more influential agent of socialization than the family.

3.2.4 Mass Media

Instrumental in making communication with large numbers of people possible, mass media provide continuity of knowledge or public information about people, events, and changes occurring in society and the threats they sometimes pose to the existing social order. Types of mass media include books, magazines, radio, television, and motion pictures.

Problem Solving Example:

Q Sociologists have found that there are many agents of socialization—persons, groups, and institutions. The family, school, peer group, and mass media are basic social institutions that supply structure in modern society. Why is the family unique among the agents of socialization?

 A Sociologists contend that, unlike the other agents of socialization, the family is a constant influence in one's life. Since one's familial relationships tend to be lifelong, the family provides a continuous frame of reference for language, social and religious customs, and social class. Additionally, the family helps children internalize their culture and parental expectations. Though the peer group and school grow in influence as the child matures, sociologists maintain that these agents never fully replace the family as the central agent of socialization. The internalized expectations from the family help to direct the behavior of the adult child.

3.3 Resocialization and the Role of Total Institution

Resocialization refers to the process of discarding behavioral practices and adopting new ones as part of a transition in life. For example, when one becomes a parent for the first time, he or she may have to perform new duties. Resocialization such as this occurs throughout our lives. Resocialization, however, can be a much more dramatic process, especially when it takes place in a total institution, such as a place of residence where persons are confined for a period of time and cut off from the rest of society. This type of resocialization involves a fundamental break with the past to allow for the rebuilding of personality and the learning of norms and values of a new, unfamiliar social environment. The environment of a total institution is deliberately controlled in order to achieve this end. Some examples of total institutions include mental hospitals, the military, and prisons.

Problem Solving Example:

Q Sara Griggs has been studying the socialization process among students as they move from elementary school to high school. She has noticed gradual changes in behavior between the male and female students, with the young men tending to be less aggressive toward the young women than they were when they were children. Sara has concluded she is witnessing resocialization among her subjects. What is resocialization? What factors may be contributing to the resocialization of these students?

A Resocialization is the process of discarding some behavioral practices and adopting new ones—based on newly learned norms and values—as part of a transition in life. In this case, the transition is from childhood to adolescence. The students entering high school are encountering new expectations from their teachers and administrators. The students' behavior is expected to conform to high-school rules. Thus, they are more likely to be self-controlled and thoughtful to one another and the faculty. They are also influenced by the behavior of their older peers, most of whom will have already matured in their attitudes toward the opposite sex.

3.4 Sigmund Freud

An Austrian physician and the founder of psychoanalysis, Sigmund Freud (1856–1939) considered biological drives to be the primary source of human activity. Freud broke down the human psychological experience into three parts with relation to these biological drives. For Freud, it is through the processes or mechanisms of identification and repression (the holding back and the hiding of one's own feelings, fearing rejection by others or by one's self for having feelings that are not acceptable) that the human personality—which is comprised of the *id*, the *ego*, and the *superego*—is formed. The *id* represents the unconscious and primal striving without specific direction or purpose. It is activated by the *pleasure principle* to demand immediate and complete gratification of biological needs. These needs must be repressed and subsequently channeled in socially acceptable directions. Without socialization the human being would be a violent, amoral, predatory animal, and organized social life would be impossible. The *ego* represents the id's opposition, the most conscious aspect of personality. Defining opportunities, the goals one strives toward, and what is "real," the ego controls and checks the id. The ego deals with the world in terms of what is possible, providing limits and direction. The ego engages in reality testing, or exploratory efforts, to determine how the world responds to one's efforts, evaluates the gratification inherent in an action, and assesses the availability of objects and persons to the id, as well as the limits to be placed on the id. The *superego* eventually forms with age and experience and governs what the ego should and should not do. It allows the individual to project his or her actions into the future in a more detached sense, meaning that while the ego may avoid perpetrating an action because of a more immediate and local consequence, the superego would limit actions further on the basis that the consequence might be felt by another person at another time. Here we would see the growth of the individual in relation to other social, cultural, and psychological influences in the environment. Thus, for Freud, behavior of the individual is a result of the collaboration of all three components of personality.

3.5   Charles Horton Cooley

An economist turned social psychologist, Charles Horton Cooley (1864–1924) theorized that the self-concept, which is formed in childhood, is reevaluated every time the person enters a new social situation. There are three stages in the process of self-formation, which Cooley referred to as "the looking-glass-self": (1) we imagine how we appear to others; (2) we wonder whether others see us in the same way as we see ourselves, and in order to find out, we observe how others react to us; and (3) we develop a conception of ourselves that is based on the judgments of others. Thus, we acquire a conception of ourselves from the "looking glass," or mirror of the reactions of others.

3.6   George Herbert Mead

An American philosopher and social psychologist, George Herbert Mead (1863–1931) is best known for his evolutionary social theory of the genesis of the mind and self. Mead's basic thesis—that a single act can best be understood as a segment of a larger social act or communicative transaction between two or more persons—made social psychology central to his philosophical approach. To describe the process whereby mind and self evolve through a continuous adjustment of the individual to himself and to others, Mead used several concepts: the "Me" is the image one forms of one's self from the standpoint of "generalized others," and the "I" is the individual's reaction to a situation as he/she sees it from his/her unique standpoint.

Mead pointed out that one outcome of socialization is the ability to anticipate the reactions of others and to adjust our behavior accordingly. We do this, Mead argues, by role-playing or learning to model the behavior of significant others, such as our parents. For example, playing "house" allows children to view the world from their parents' perspectives.

3.7   Erving Goffman

Like other sociologists, Erving Goffman (1922–1983) considered the self to be a reflection of others—the cluster of roles or expectations of the people with whom one is involved at that point in the life course. It is the product of a series of encounters through which we manage the impression that others receive to convince them that we are who we claim to be. In every role we undertake, there is a virtual self waiting to be carried out. Goffman used the term *role distance* to describe the gap that exists between who we truly are and who we portray ourselves to be.

3.8   Jean Piaget

Based on experiments with children playing and responding to questions, Swiss psychologist Jean Piaget (1896–1980) proposed a theory of cognitive development that describes the changes that occur over time in the ways children think, understand, and evaluate a situation. Piaget not only stressed the part that social life plays in becoming conscious of one's own mind but, more broadly speaking, he also observed that cognitive development does not occur automatically. A given stage of cognitive development cannot be reached unless confronted with real-life experiences that foster such development. In the *sensorimotor stage*, infants are unable to differentiate themselves from their environments. They are unaware that their actions produce results, and they lack the understanding that objects exist separate from the direct and immediate experience of touching, looking, sucking, and listening.

Through sensory experience and physical contact with their environment, infants begin to experience their surroundings differently. The world becomes a relatively stable place, no longer simply the shifting chaos it is first perceived to be. In the *preoperational stage*, children begin to use language and other symbols. Not only do they begin to attach meaning to the world, they also are able to differentiate fantasy from reality. Unable to grasp an idea generally, children have no conception of weight, size, or volume (i.e., beyond the particular instance).

In the *concrete operational stage*, children make great strides in their use of logic to understand the world and how it operates. They begin to think in logical terms, to make the connection between cause and effect, and they are capable of attaching meaning or significance to a particular event. Although they cannot conceive of an idea beyond the concrete situation or event, they have begun to imagine themselves in the position of another and thus to grasp a situation from the other's point of view. In effect, it is during this stage of cognitive development that the foundation for engaging in more complex activities with others (such as role-playing) is laid. Finally, in the *formal operational stage,* children develop the capacity for thinking in highly abstract terms of metaphors and hypotheses which may or may not be based in reality.

Problem Solving Example:

Q As described by Jean Piaget, the cognitive development of children grows in stages relative to and determined by their direct experiences in negotiating life. One of these stages is the formal operational stage. What, according to Piaget, occurs in this stage?

A Formal operational thinkers can handle hypothetical problems. They are, for instance, able to project themselves into the future and think about long-term goals. Scientific reasoning is also possible, that is, the ability to isolate a problem, review it systematically, and figure out all possible solutions. The formal thinker is capable of understanding and appreciating the symbolic abstractions of algebra and literary criticism, as well as the use of metaphors in literature. Formal operations, therefore, involve the development of logical and systematic thinking.

Piaget believed that cognitive development proceeded through four stages and that the order in which children pass through these stages does not vary, though the rate at which they develop does vary from child to child. Piaget wrote that each stage of cognitive development represents a qualitatively different way of thinking. That is, children in each stage think differently from children in other stages. Therefore, it is not just that children acquire more information as they grow older, but that how they think actually changes with age. Children pass from one stage to another as a result of biological maturity and experiences in the environment.

In the sensorimotor stage (the first 18 to 24 months), children think as a result of coordination of sensory input and motor responses. Because the child has not developed language, intelligence is non-verbal or nonsymbolic (the child cannot mentally represent objects or events). Piaget was the first to suggest that infants lack this ability.

In the preoperational stage (from 2 to 7 years old), they can now symbolize or mentally represent their world. This stage is dominated by a rapid development in language, which is a form of symbolic thinking. Limitations at this stage include *irreversibility* (the inability to mentally reverse a physical action to return an object to its original state), *centration* (the tendency to focus on one detail in the situation to the neglect of important features), and *egocentrism* (the inability to consider another's viewpoint). These limitations are used to describe why preoperational children cannot solve conservation tasks. Children might believe that when you pour water from a tall, thin glass to a short, fat one you have less water. In the concrete operational stage (ages 7 to 12), children will see that the amount of water stays the same. They de-center their attention and understand reversibility. Children can arrange objects by size and weight and can divide something into its parts. Math skills develop at this stage, but children can only apply their knowledge to concrete objects and events. They have not yet learned to think hypothetically. That occurs in the final stage, formal operational.

Criticisms of Piaget's theory include his underestimation of children's cognitive abilities. Studies have shown that children are capable of performing many tasks (e.g., conservation) at earlier stages than Piaget predicted. Piaget also paid little attention to individual differences. Some aspects of his theory (e.g., formal operational) may be culturally specific.

3.9   Erik Erikson

Departing from Freud's emphasis on childhood and instinct, Erik Erikson (1902–1994) delineated eight stages of psychosocial development where *ego identity*, the sense of continuity and sameness in the conception one has of one's self that does not change over time or situation; *ego development*, the potential for change and growth that exists over the course of a person's life; and the *social environment* are involved. They are:

Stage 1—the nurturing stage in which a child's sense of either basic trust or mistrust is established.

Stage 2—there emerges the feeling of autonomy or feelings of doubt and shame from not being able to handle the situations one encounters in life.

Stage 3—the child develops either a sense of initiative and self-confidence or feelings of guilt depending on how successful he or she is in exploring the environment and in dealing with peers.

Stage 4—the focus shifts from family to school where the child develops a conception of him- or herself as being industrious or inferior.

Stage 5—failure to establish a clear and firm sense of one's self results in the person's becoming confused about his or her identity.

Stage 6—one meets or fails to meet the challenge presented by young adulthood of forming stable relationships, the outcome being either "intimacy or isolation and loneliness."

Stage 7—a person's contribution to the well-being of others through citizenship, work, and family becomes self-generative, and hence, that person's fulfilling of the primary tasks of mature adulthood is complete.

Stage 8—the developmental challenge posed by the knowledge that one is reaching the end is to find a sense of continuity and meaning, to break the sense of isolation and self-absorption that the thought of one's impending death produces, thereby yielding to despair.

3.10 Lawrence Kohlberg

Piaget's work inspired Lawrence Kohlberg (1927–1987) to research the development of children as moral philosophers by conducting a series of longitudinal and cross-cultural studies extending over several decades. Kohlberg concluded that given the proper experience and stimulation, children go through a sequence of six stages of moral reasoning. These stages are paired off to form three levels: pre-conventional, conventional, and post-conventional.

In the pre-conventional level (between ages four and ten), a child's sense of good and bad is connected with the fear of being punished for disobeying those in positions of power. Stages 1 and 2 occur at this level. In Stage 1 (the punishment and obedience orientation), the child learns that actions have consequences. The motivation switches from avoiding punishment to satisfying a need (usually their own). A child's motivation may also include the exchange of favors (do for me and I do for you).

During adolescence the conventional level begins. A child's conformity to the rules becomes connected with the belief that the existing social order must ultimately be the right and true order and, therefore, ought to be followed. Stages 3 and 4 are reached at this level. Stage 3 is defined by the need for acceptance in interpersonal relationships. The motivating factor for a child is gaining approval and avoiding rejection. Stage 4 is law and order orientation. Judgments at this stage are based on acceptance of and respect for authority. Adolescents concern themselves with doing one's duty for society and gaining the approval of a true authority figure.

Finally, at the post-conventional level, action and self-judgment among older children and young adults are guided by considerations of the welfare of the community, of the rights of the individual, and of universal ethical principles, such as justice, equality, and individual dignity. At Stage 5 (social contract/legalistic orientation), moral judgment is motivated by respect for others and for the social order. Stage 6 is marked by the understanding of the universality of ethics. Right behavior is defined with respect to the inherent dignity of human beings as individuals. Kohlberg has been criticized for basing his model of human development on the male experience, having assumed that women and girls are incapable of reaching the highest stages of moral reasoning.

3.11 Carol Gilligan

Taking Kohlberg to task on this point, Carol Gilligan, the current Chair of Harvard's Gender Studies doctoral program, found by comparison that women bring a different set of values to their judgments of right and wrong. For instance, whereas males approached the moral problem of whether or not it is wrong to steal to save the life of a dying wife in terms of the ethic of ultimate ends, females approached the same problem from the standpoint of an ethic of responsibility by wondering what the consequences of the moral decision to steal or not to steal would be for the child, the husband, the entire family—the goal being to find the best solution for everyone involved.

In effect, their different approaches to resolving the problem can be explained by the different roles women have in our society as compared with men. Thus, Gilligan concludes there is no essential difference between the inner workings of the psyches of boys and girls.

Quiz: Socialization

1. According to Freud's theories, the _____ is the most conscious aspect of the personality, defining opportunities and setting goals.

    (A) ego

    (B) id

    (C) superego

    (D) self-concept

    (E) "me-self"

2. According to Erikson, the process of establishing a clear and firm sense of one's self results in the person's continuous development of his or her

    (A) heritage.

    (B) ethnicity.

    (C) race.

    (D) identity.

    (E) sex.

3. The process of becoming human in the sense of being able to participate in society is the process of

    (A) transformation.

    (B) maturation.

    (C) inculcation.

    (D) exhibition.

    (E) socialization.

4. The family is considered the most important agent of socialization until _____ begins.

    (A) maturation

    (B) rebellion

    (C) schooling

    (D) puberty

    (E) None of the above.

5. Gilligan's study of moral reasoning among females was a response to the work of

    (A) Jean Piaget.

    (B) Erik Erikson.

    (C)   Sigmund Freud.

    (D)   George Herbert Mead.

    (E)   Lawrence Kohlberg.

6.   The term Goffman used to describe the gap between who we are and who we portray ourselves to be is

    (A)   role conflict.

    (B)   role strain.

    (C)   cognitive dissonance.

    (D)   role distance.

    (E)   None of the above.

7.   The process of discarding behavior practices and adopting new ones as part of a transition in life is called

    (A)   indoctrination.

    (B)   maturation.

    (C)   resocialization.

    (D)   incarceration.

    (E)   experimentation.

8.   Kohlberg took a longitudinal and cross-cultural approach to his investigation of the development of _____ reasoning in children.

    (A)   moral

    (B)   social

    (C)   spiritual

    (D)   economic

    (E)   None of the above.

9.   Which theorist proposed that pretending to be other people is central to the development of a self-concept by young children?

   (A)   Sigmund Freud

   (B)   George Herbert Mead

   (C)   Karl Marx

   (D)   Emile Durkheim

   (E)   Erving Goffman

10.   Piaget observed that real-life experiences were crucial to _____ development.

   (A)   emotional

   (B)   critical

   (C)   political

   (D)   economic

   (E)   cognitive

ANSWER KEY

1.	(A)	6.	(D)
2.	(D)	7.	(C)
3.	(E)	8.	(A)
4.	(C)	9.	(B)
5.	(E)	10.	(E)

CHAPTER 4

Defining Culture

4.1 Culture

With society as the reference point, culture is generally defined as a blueprint according to which the members of a society or a group go about their daily lives. Culture consists of the common (i.e., learned and shared) social heritage of beliefs, customs, skills, traditions, and knowledge that members pass on to one another.

With the reference point being nothing more than individuals communicating meaning and value to one another, culture represents all things made (all objects of thought and experience), material (as in the tools we use), and nonmaterial (as in the rules people live by, the ideals according to which people live, the ideas in terms of which we think). Social structure represents the ways in which individuals have come to organize themselves internally and externally. Socialization is never complete. Deviance is very much a part of how human beings live and work as members of a community or organization.

4.2 Material and Nonmaterial Culture

Culture is comprised of material and nonmaterial elements. Material culture consists of the things to which people attach meaning and use. Items of material culture include cars, clothing, books, and burial sites. Nonmaterial culture (which includes languages, ideas, belief systems, rules, customs, and political systems) consists of the abstract terms that human beings create for the purposes of defining, describing, explaining, clarifying, ordering, organizing, and communicating what they do and how they live.

In this context, a symbol does not merely refer to "the representation of one thing by another." Many primates can be conditioned to make certain associations or to learn what certain verbal cues mean, but only human beings create symbols. A symbol represents something to which a certain meaning or value is attached by the person or persons who use it. All human languages, therefore, represent complex symbol systems through which thoughts are expressed but not determined. Culture includes the tools we use, the rules we live by, the ideals to which we are committed, and the ideas that we express.

Problem Solving Example:

 Tools, rules, and ideas describe elements of culture. What is culture?

Culture consists of the defining elements which characterize a specific group or society. This includes beliefs, customs, skills, use of specific tools, traditions, and other practices that are passed down from generation to generation. Sociologists go on to define culture as all things made, both material and nonmaterial; that is, all objects of thought and experience, all tools, rules, ideals, and ideas by which people live. These represent the ways individuals organize themselves internally and externally. Cultural elements would include religious beliefs and rituals, marriage and childbearing practices, instruments used in farming or warfare, rules governing disputes between neighbors, and commonly held attitudes concerning hard labor and recreation.

4.3 Aspects of Culture

Culture, thus, includes the symbols, sounds, events, and objects to which people attach meaning and significance.

4.3.1 Symbols and Language

Unlike other animals, man alone is capable of making sense of what he sees around him by using symbols to organize and communicate his observations. One form of communication that is unique to human beings is spoken language. Human language is unlike the various types of communications used by other species that make use of sounds, smells, and body gestures.

4.3.2 Norms and Values

Norms are the rules or expectations with which people govern themselves, formally or informally, or to which people orient their behavior. They exist in order to create social control. Values express the ideas or central beliefs common to the members of a group describing what they consider good, right, and desirable and against which the norms of a particular group or subgroup may be judged.

Values represent not only the things that give meaning and about which human beings feel certain, but also the ideas that make such things so important that humans are willing to fight, work, or give up something of their own in exchange for their preservation.

In this context, norms are binding rules whose violation results in some form of punishment.

4.3.3 Folkways and Mores

Folkways and mores are two different strengths or degrees of norms, the latter being more deserving of punishment when broken. Folkways are the usual customs and conventions of everyday life. Members of a society or group generally expect each other to conform to folkways, but do not insist upon such conformity. Nonconformists are thought to be peculiar or eccentric, particularly if they consistently violate such norms. Folkways differ from values in that they lack a moral component. For example, eating dessert before dinner is a violation of a traditional folkway, but invites less, if any, sanctioning than a violation of mores.

Mores are norms of such moral and ethical significance to the members of a society or community that their violation is regarded as a serious matter worthy of strong criticism, anger, punishment, or institutionalization. Violation of mores, such as our culture's prohibition of incest, will result in severe sanctioning, and will bring about responses of revulsion, as these norms guide extremely serious matters in society.

Problem Solving Example:

Q Sharon wants to compare the socialization of Protestant and Catholic women in the rural South. She wants to know whether young Protestant women generally make different choices about marriage than young Catholic women. Sharon has a choice of studying either the women's everyday customs or their core beliefs. Which would provide Sharon with the best information to determine whether differences between the two groups of women exist? Why?

A Though both choices would reveal something about the culture of the women being studied, customs are based on daily, practical considerations and are, therefore, much more likely to be similar between groups living in the same area. Everyday customs demonstrate the young women's practices, but customs and folkways lack the moral component of values, whereas core beliefs represent the highest ideals for each group. Adherence to these ideals demonstrates one's conformity to group standards and is likely to be key to one's inclusion in the group. Monumental differences in ideology usually generate the social splintering of groups that results in the formation of subcultures and countercultures (see Section 4.5). Members of a group do expect others in the group to conform to folkways, but nonconformity to these conventions is not likely to be grounds for sanction.

If Sharon conducts her study based on the day-to-day customs of these women, she would learn what activities are similar or different in their everyday lives and the types of decisions they make about the future, but she would not gain an understanding of what tenets lead them to these choices. A study of core beliefs would reveal this.

For instance, Sharon might discover that Protesant women would be more likely to marry outside of their religion than Catholic women, based on the belief that a man's moral character is more important than his religious affiliation, while Catholic women might believe it is more important to marry within the Catholic Church.

4.3.4 Cultural Universals

Cultural universals are the basic elements essential to individual and collective survival that are found to exist in all cultures. Food, water, and shelter are cultural universals.

4.3.5 Cultural Variability

Cultural variability (or cultural variation) refers to the variety of methods different groups have devised to meet the same needs. For example, some societies meet the need for food by hunting and gathering; others meet that need by planting crops and raising domesticated animals.

4.4 Cultural Diversity

The diversity to be found among human cultures can lead to ethnocentrism. Ethnocentrism refers not only to the attitude that one's own cultural or ethnic values are the only good and true values, but also refers to the tendency to judge other cultures by one's own standards. Taken to extremes, ethnocentrism can lead to stagnation within a culture by excluding outside influences and limiting the growth of that culture. Ethnocentrism also poses a problem for sociologists, as their own cultural biases can affect how they interpret the ways and beliefs of a society or culture they are studying. Cultural relativism refers to social scientists' efforts to be objective in their observations, either by not imposing their own meanings on the events being observed, or by focusing solely on the reasons why elements exist.

4.5 Subcultures and Countercultures

In today's world, cultures generally represent nations or nation-states, each with its own cultural identity. Nations, however, tend to consist of relatively large segments or subcultures which, though not wholly separate from the larger culture, represent unique cultures and cultural organizations unto themselves. The Amish are one example of a subculture that has been able to preserve its traditional mode of organizing work within farming communities despite America's high level of industrialization.

All cultures are concerned with the issues of preserving their values, beliefs, language, and lifestyles. Thus, countercultures (whose values, beliefs, and ways of life do not conform to the norm) can pose a threat to their existence and survival. Distinctive values and norms, as well as unconventional behavior, may characterize a counterculture. Examples of countercultures include the Ku Klux Klan and other white supremacist groups, as well as some cults.

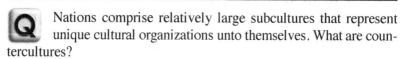

Problem Solving Example:

Q Nations comprise relatively large subcultures that represent unique cultural organizations unto themselves. What are countercultures?

A Countercultures differ from subcultures in that they not only pursue, but promote values and norms in opposition to those of the dominant culture, which seeks to maintain its established beliefs and customs. The Amish are a subculture because, although they sustain a separate way of life, they do not seek to impress it upon others. In contrast, the "hippies" of the 1960s were a counterculture because they often actively protested the actions and beliefs of the establishment in an effort to bring about a change in society.

Quiz: Defining Culture

1. John is introduced to Fred, and the two of them shake hands. This handshaking ritual is best characterized as a

    (A)   more.

    (B)   taboo.

    (C)   law.

    (D)   folkway.

    (E)   sanction.

2. Jewish Americans, police officers, and college students could all be characterized as members of

    (A)   countercultures.

    (B)   subcultures.

    (C)   ethnic groups.

    (D)   racial groups.

    (E)   social classes.

3. The concept of culture includes all of the following EXCEPT

    (A)   personal values.

    (B)   religious beliefs.

    (C)   styles of dress.

    (D)   family organization.

    (E)   individual intelligence.

4. _____ describe to members of the group what is good, right, and desirable.

    (A)   Values

    (B)   Norms

(C) Folkways

(D) Mores

(E) Symbols

5. The concept that one's own cultural or ethnic values are the only good and true values is known by sociologists as

(A) bias.

(B) socialization.

(C) diversity.

(D) ethnocentrism.

(E) egocentrism.

6. The one form of communication unique to human beings is

(A) body language.

(B) gestures.

(C) facial expression.

(D) spoken language.

(E) smells.

7. In Boston, an Irish-American community exists, complete with a distinctive religion and ethnic lifestyle. This group can be categorized as a(n)

(A) counterculture.

(B) nonmaterial culture.

(C) subculture.

(D) eccentric culture.

(E) deviant subculture.

8. To members of society, violations of _____ are worthy of strong criticism, anger, punishment, or institutionalization.

(A) laws

    (B) norms

    (C) mores

    (D) folkways

    (E) None of the above.

9.   Rules or expectations that govern our behavior are

    (A) values.

    (B) folkways.

    (C) mores.

    (D) laws.

    (E) norms.

10. Basic elements essential to individuals across cultures are called

    (A) mores.

    (B) habits.

    (C) principles.

    (D) laws.

    (E) universals.

ANSWER KEY

1.	(D)	6.	(D)
2.	(B)	7.	(C)
3.	(E)	8.	(C)
4.	(A)	9.	(E)
5.	(D)	10.	(E)

CHAPTER 5

Defining Society

5.1 Society

In the broadest sense possible, society refers to human association (i.e., to the presence of a connecting link between human beings). In that sense, any number of people interacting in ways that form a pattern or any social relationship formed on the basis of common meaning(s) would constitute a "society." More narrowly defined, a society is a relatively permanent grouping of people living in the same geographic area who are economically self-sufficient, politically independent, and who share a common culture.

5.2 Sociocultural Evolution

From the standpoint of society as a system, the concept of sociocultural evolution refers to the tendency of society (like other living organisms) to become more complex over time.

5.3 Types of Societies

The ecological approach, which focuses on how much variation in cultural and social elements of the system can be attributed to the environment, provides the foundation for classifying societies.

5.3.1 Hunting and Gathering

Hunting and gathering societies, whose economies are based on hunting animals and gathering vegetation, have largely disappeared, with the exception of a few tribes in Africa and Malaysia. Most of these societies are nomadic, meaning that as animal and vegetation sources are depleted, they must move in pursuit of food.

5.3.2 Horticultural and Pastoral

Horticultural and pastoral societies are characterized by the domestication of animals and the use of hand tools to cultivate plants. With the use of a hoe and other digging materials, such as sticks, groups were able to gather their food source from one area. In places where crops were difficult to grow, domesticated animals were more often used. It is during this period that we see a material surplus among some horticultural and pastoral societies due to the fact that the work of a few could support many. People could produce more than they could use.

5.3.3 Agricultural

Agricultural societies are more complex than horticultural and pastoral societies in the level of technology used to support crops and livestock. With the advent of irrigation and the use of draft animals, farmers could produce a large surplus.

5.3.4 Industrial

In industrial societies, complex machinery and energy sources (rather than humans and other animals) are used for production. During this period there emerged the use of automobiles, trains, and electronic communication, such as radios, telephones, and televisions.

5.3.5 Postindustrial

Unlike industrial societies, in which the primary form of production centers around machine-generated material goods, post-industrial societies create, process, and store information.

5.4   Theories of Society

Karl Marx, Emile Durkheim, and Max Weber all approached the concept of society from varying perspectives with concentrations on division of labor, class struggles, sociological order, biological needs, and industrial and religious differences. Each social theorist provided new avenues of thought for students of sociology.

5.4.1 Karl Marx—On History, Class Strugles, and Alienation

German philosopher and social theorist Karl Marx (1818–1883) believed that all of human history and society can be traced to the basic material circumstance of men and women in a productive relationship with nature. Originally, wholly communal individuals engaged in producing the means of subsistence as members of a tribe or family; human beings were seen as naturally dividing their labor.

In the simplest type of society, the division of labor, however wide, is minimal, based on the different productive roles (or relations with nature) of the different sexes. With the progressive differentiation or occupational specialization accompanying the division of labor comes the capacity to produce a surplus beyond that which is necessary to satisfy basic human needs. The production of a surplus allows for the exchange of goods, a situation in which human beings have become increasingly individualized. Thus, communal property is replaced by private property in the means of production.

With that, classes and class struggles emerge, and the class struggle characterizing "the history of all hitherto existing societies" begins to take its course. When the class system became so simplified as to leave only two classes (capitalist owners and working proletariat) to fight it out, Marx predicted that this would soon end in a successful workers' revolution that would eliminate private property.

Thus, although Marx himself never completely defined the term "class," his use of the term suggests not only a "group" of people who have in common a certain relationship to the means of production, but also an organization of society based on class relations that link the economic relations in production to all other relations in society.

Problem Solving Example:

Q Michael has been studying the works of the early sociologist Karl Marx. He has found Marx's perspective on social structures most intriguing and in line with his own. How might Michael describe his perspective on social structures in light of Marxist theory?

A Michael believes that social institutions create and maintain an unequal division between the working class and the investor class and, furthermore, that these two groups are constantly struggling for power. This is the essence of Marxist conflict theory of social structure. Marx contended that class struggles were part of all industrialized societies. Marx believed that industrial workers would revolt, defeating the owners of the means of production and eliminating personal property. Additionally, he believed that class differences were created and sustained by industrialization and that absorption of the working class into the bourgeoisie was not possible. Because Marx never completely defined "class," other scholars have challenged the general soundness of his theories (See Marx, *Capital,* 1867, and *The German Ideology,* 1845).

5.4.2 Emile Durkheim—On Social Facts and Human Nature

French sociologist Emile Durkheim (1858–1917) laid the foundation for what has become one of the leading approaches to American sociology today by demanding a separate existence for the science of sociology on the grounds that it has both an object and a substratum exclusively its own. The object is social facts, patterned regularities known through statistics to describe the collectivity as distinct from the individuals of which it is comprised, and the substratum is none other than society as a whole.

The logical starting point for comprehending Durkheim's conception of society is the problem of order. Durkheim believed that if one could conceive of man in a state of nature, there would be no restraints upon his aspirations, no limits on his insatiable desires, and, therefore, no possibility of a moral life. Thus, without the framework of a body of rules regulating interactions, conflict would be inevitable.

Comparing man in a state of nature to other animals, Durkheim concluded that not only is man different from other animals in that he is not satiated once his biological needs are met, but that man is also like other animals because, in a state of nature, his life has no meaning, rationale, or purpose outside of itself. Based on this conclusion, Durkheim argued that society is the source of both moral life and mental life in that it sufficiently limits our insatiable desires and gives meaning to our lives.

The structure of society solidifies, and the process of society integrates most individuals within its orbit into the whole. For instance, Durkheim reasoned that Protestantism was a less strongly integrated church than Catholicism because it permitted the individual greater freedom of thought and judgment and had fewer common beliefs and practices. Durkheim attributed religious ideas concerning the ultimate meaning of life to the collective group or societal experience.

Problem Solving Examples:

Q Jawad wonders whether students at his university, who presumably would have greater access to information on the hazards of smoking, are less inclined to begin smoking than their peers who are not enrolled in the university. Keeping in mind Durkheim's concept of social facts, what research strategy would best provide Jawad with the information he is seeking?

A Keeping in mind that Durkheim's concept of social facts relates to patterns of behavior of the group and not the individual, Jawad should concentrate his efforts on measuring the behavior of the collective, rather than the individual. Jawad should draw a random sample of university students, survey them on their smoking habits, and compare the data from his survey with data on members of the general (or non-university) population roughly within the age range of those in the university population.

Q The French sociologist Emile Durkheim studied the relationship of religion and social structures. How did Durkheim compare Protestantism and Catholicism?

A Durkheim concluded that Protestantism was a less cohesive religion than Catholicism. For example, Durkheim argued that the religious ceremonies and rituals of Catholicism reinforced collective values and strengthened conformity among the individuals. Protestantism permitted believers greater freedom of thought and judgment and had fewer common beliefs and practices than Catholicism. In his work *The Elementary Forms of Religion* (1912), Durkheim contends that religion is founded on social structure. In fact, the individual's morality is a construct of society.

5.4.3 Max Weber—On Verstehen, the Ideal Type, and Rationalization

German sociologist Max Weber (1864–1920) conducted a series of investigations of culture in China, India, Greece, Rome, the Middle East, and the West in an attempt to explain why certain phenomena are unique to Western civilization. For instance, why did the Industrial Revolution originate in Great Britain and not, as one might expect, in China, which was already a country of large walled cities in times prehistoric by our conception? Stressing the factors that distinguish a particular culture from Western civilization, Weber applied the methods of *Verstehen*, or understanding the meanings others attach to their actions, to arrive at a causal explanation of the fact that, in the universal history of culture, no other civilization entered the path of rationalization unique to the West. This path led Western society from traditional to rational action. Rationalization is the practical application of knowledge to achieve a desired end and the process by which every feature of human behavior becomes subject to calculation, measurement, and control.

Over the course of his investigations, Weber developed and employed the concept of *ideal type*. Ideal type is a way of describing the basic features of a particular social phenomenon: for example, bureaucracy (see Section 7.7.1). While this model is not meant to be a realistic picture of all such institutions, it can be used as a standard against which institutions are compared and their differences and similarities measured. Weber also applied reason to his studies and, wherever necessary, made use of the uncertain procedure of the imaginary experiment (of thinking away elements in a causal chain of motivation). In the process, he found religious differences that explain why the same course of development in China and elsewhere was not possible. More precisely, he found the Protestant ethic, the sacred value placed on all work in this world as a calling set by God, as well as saving and investment as further concrete proof of salvation, to be decisive in producing the spirit of the modern form of industrial capitalism. The Protestant ethic gave Western culture religious sanction to abandon traditional ways and turn its efforts toward the rational pursuit of wealth. Non-Western cultures were lacking this incentive to change.

In effect, Weber determined that understanding (as the specific character of sociological knowledge) may be of two sorts. The first is the immediate comprehension of an act or an idea one has observed, e.g., as in our direct grasp of the statement $1 + 1 = 2$. The second is the comprehension of the meaning underlying an action by intellectually grasping the sequence of motivation within the social context of the shared meanings of the action—in other words, understanding the meanings others attach to their own actions.

Quiz: Defining Society

1. The domestication of animals and the use of hand tools to cultivate plants characterize what early societies?

    (A) Nomadic

    (B) Primitive

    (C) Horticultural and pastoral

    (D) Agricultural

    (E) None of the above.

2. Sociologists have noted the accumulation of _____ in these societies as people became able to produce more than they could use.

    (A) disease

    (B) spoilage

    (C) war

    (D) surplus

    (E) family

3. The patterned regularities that describe the collectivity as distinct from the individuals of which it is comprised are known as

    (A) statistics.

    (B) society.

    (C) socialization.

    (D) social facts.

    (E) social laws.

4. Irrigation and draft animals characterize _____ societies.

    (A) hunting and gathering

    (B) agricultural

    (C) industrial

    (D) postindustrial

    (E) nomadic

5. Societies that exist on nondomesticated animal and vegetation sources are quite often _____; they must move in pursuit of food.

    (A) ineffective

    (B) short-lived

    (C) healthier

    (D) nomadic

    (E) primitive

6.   The storage of _____ is one characteristic of the postindustrial society.

    (A) information

    (B) surplus

    (C) weapons

    (D) currency

    (E) None of the above.

7.   The term given to a relatively permanent grouping of people living in the same geographic area who are economically self-sufficient, politically independent, and who share a common culture is

    (A) peer group.

    (B) society.

    (C) subculture.

    (D) family.

    (E) culture.

8.   Automobiles, trains, radios, telephones, and televisions evolved during the time of _____ societies.

    (A) post-war

    (B) feudal

    (C) agricultural

    (D) horticultural

    (E) industrial

9. Societies tend to become more complex over time. This is referred to as sociocultural

    (A) maturation.

    (B) growth.

    (C) sophistication.

    (D) evolution.

    (E) None of the above.

10. Weber referred to the sacred value placed on all work in this world as a calling set by God as

    (A) social order.

    (B) faith.

    (C) morality.

    (D) piety.

    (E) Protestant ethic.

ANSWER KEY

1.	(C)	6.	(A)
2.	(D)	7.	(B)
3.	(D)	8.	(E)
4.	(B)	9.	(D)
5.	(D)	10.	(E)

CHAPTER 6

Defining Social Interaction

6.1 Social Interaction

Consistent with Weber's view of society, every culture has a structure that can be described and analyzed. This structure represents the multitude of shared values, shared beliefs, and common expectations of a particular culture around which people have organized their lives. This structure also leads to a certain degree of predictability in human affairs.

6.2 Social Structure, Society, and Social Systems

Consistent with a view of society as a continuing number of people living in the same region in a relatively permanent unit, social structure is the way in which people's relations in society are arranged to form a network. They are relatively organized in the sense that there is thought to be some degree of structure and system to the patterns of social interaction of which any society is composed.

Contrary then to the latter definition, "society" here does not represent a whole. The structure is thought to be composed of similar elements of statuses (positions in a society or in a group), roles (the behavior of people occupying particular positions), groups (units each with a number of people interacting with one another in ways that form a pattern and who are united by the feeling of being bound together by "a consciousness of kind"), and institutions (organized systems of social relationships that emerge in response to the basic problems or needs of every society).

In terms of society constituting more than one system, social structure consists of the patterns of interaction formed by the enactment of culture (the map for living in a society). The social structure is thought to be composed of multiple systems or institutions—each considered a total system unto itself—in addition to several other types of components. It is argued that there are certain elements that are necessary to both individual and collective survival. When these elements become organized into institutional spheres, they form society's economic system, political structure, family system, educational process, and belief system.

Besides being determined by the social context of statuses and roles, behavior is also thought to be largely determined by the definition of the situation (the process whereby we define, explain, and evaluate the social context of the situations in which we find ourselves before deciding which behavior and attitudes are appropriate). Each system forms an arrangement or structure of statuses and roles existing apart from their occupants.

6.3 Status

Status may refer to a position in society and/or in a group.

6.3.1 Ascribed Status

An ascribed status is automatically conferred on a person with no effort made or no choice involved on his or her part, such as race or sex. An ascribed status is involuntarily assumed—for example, being Native American, a son, or a widower.

6.3.2 Achieved Status

The opposite of ascribed status, achieved status is assumed largely through one's own doings or efforts. Examples of achieved status include being a spouse, a rock star, an "A" student, or an engineering major.

6.3.3   Master Status

Master status is the status with which a person is most identified. It is the most important status that a person holds, not only because it affects almost every aspect of the person's life, but also because of its general symbolic value. People take for granted that a person holding such a position possesses other traits associated with it. Examples of master status would be man, woman, or president.

6.3.4   Status Set

A status set consists of all the statuses that a person occupies. All of us occupy a number of statuses simultaneously. A woman may be a mother to her children, a wife to her husband, a professor to her students, and a colleague to her co-workers. The statuses of mother, wife, professor, and colleague together form the status set of this woman.

Problem Solving Example:

Q Kathy is a sociology student at a small Midwestern college. She is a single mother and works part-time at a department store. What is Kathy's social status set?

A Because a "status set" is composed of all of the positions a person occupies in society, Kathy's status set is student, mother, and worker. Status is a position in society or in a group. Ascribed status is automatically assigned to a person with no effort made by the individual—for example, race and gender are ascribed statuses. Achieved status is that which an individual, such as Kathy, has assumed through his or her own efforts; for example, mother, worker, and college student.

6.4   Roles

Role refers to what a person does (i.e., the part one plays or how one is expected to behave) by virtue of occupying a particular status or position.

STATUS

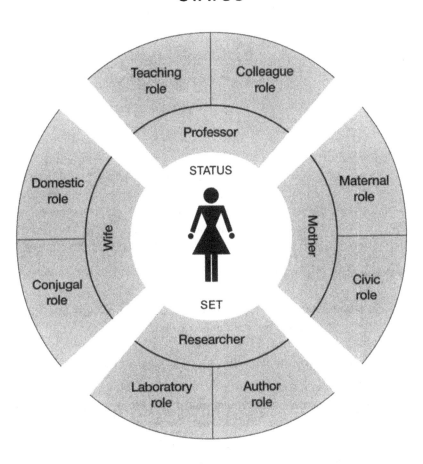

SET

Figure 6.1 Status Set

Every status and role is accompanied by a set of norms or role expectations describing behavioral expectations, or the limits of what people occupying the position are expected to do and how they are expected to do it. For example, the role of a mother is socially accepted as one of a nurturing, loving, and responsible nature. There are thought to be marked differences and, thus, extensive variations in how a particular role is played out, depending on differences in how those holding a particular position define their role. In effect, group differences and the conflicts they generate are thought to continually transform the system and structure.

6.4.1 Role Strain

Role strain refers to a situation where different and conflicting expectations exist with regard to a particular status. For example, a professor may enjoy his students and may socialize outside of class with them. At the same time, though, he is responsible for ascertaining that their performance is up to par and that they attend class regularly. To achieve this end, he may have to distance himself from his students.

6.4.2 Role Conflict

Role conflict occurs when a person occupies multiple statuses that contradict one another. For example, a teacher whose own child is in his or her class cannot always play the role of parent, but must abort parental tendencies and play the role of teacher to the child while in the classroom.

Problem Solving Example:

Social roles are interchangeable and highly predictable from person to person. Offer a challenge to this statement.

Because social roles are defined by the individual and by the expectations of the group to which the individual holding the role belongs, sociologists believe there are extensive variations in how a particular role is played out. They are neither interchangeable nor highly predictable. For example, the expected behaviors associated with being a high-school teacher might vary depending on whether the teacher works in a large city high school or a small private school, or tutors a single student.

Quiz: Defining Social Interaction

1. Sociologically, a master status means

    (A) the relationship an employer has to his or her employees.

    (B) the status of an artisan or craftsman in society.

    (C) the status that touches every aspect of a person's life and is the most prominent and consistent part of his or her identity.

    (D) the status that a person strives to achieve.

    (E) None of the above.

2. Which of the following lists of characteristics best illustrates ascribed statuses?

    (A) Female, Asian, Olympic athlete

    (B) Male, Jewish, rabbi

    (C) Female, married, pregnant

    (D) Female, age 27, pediatrician

    (E) Male, African American, age 45

3. Regarding the distinction made in sociology between status and role, which is the most accurate statement?

    (A) Status refers to a social position; role refers to behavior patterns, obligations, and privileges associated with a social position.

(B) Role refers to a position one holds in society; status refers to how much money one has in the social position.

(C) Status refers to behavior; role refers to a position in society.

(D) There is no difference; they mean the same thing.

(E) Status refers to the social position designated by birth; role refers to the social position which can be achieved.

4. A professor has certain rights and obligations associated with his or her status, such as meeting with students and preparing lectures. These rights and obligations associated with a status are known as

(A) master statuses.

(B) ascribed statuses.

(C) achieved statuses.

(D) roles.

(E) impression management.

5. George is a college student. He also works 25 hours a week to support his wife and small child. He is having a hard time pleasing his boss and keeping his grades up. A sociologist would say that George is suffering from

(A) role ambiguity.

(B) role conflict.

(C) role strain.

(D) role performance.

(E) role playing.

6. The complex arrangement of people's relations in a society is a

    (A) peer group.

    (B) community.

    (C) family.

    (D) support group.

    (E) social network.

7. Status that is assumed largely through one's doings or efforts is called _____ status.

    (A) mobility

    (B) class

    (C) esteemed

    (D) inherited

    (E) achieved

8. The name given to the concept of positions in a society or group is

    (A) role.

    (B) status.

    (C) class.

    (D) group.

    (E) None of the above.

9. The combined statuses a person occupies are that person's

    (A) life outcome.

    (B) status set.

    (C) status outcome.

    (D) master status.

    (E) None of the above.

10. When a particular status includes different and simultaneously demanding expectations, that status is said to contain _____ strain.

    (A) role

    (B) position

    (C) status

    (D) power

    (E) class

ANSWER KEY

1.	(C)	6.	(E)
2.	(E)	7.	(E)
3.	(A)	8.	(B)
4.	(D)	9.	(B)
5.	(B)	10.	(A)

CHAPTER 7

Groups and

Organizations

7.1 Social Groups and Relationships

Strictly speaking, a group is an assembly of people or things. However, not all people who are assembled together are thought to constitute human or social groupings. The members of a group are considered united generally through interaction, more specifically by the relationships they share, or in particular by the quality or specific character of the relationships between the individuals of which that group is composed. In theory, any specific group represents no more than a relationship of "individual" persons.

7.2 Associations and Communal Relationships

An association is a type of relationship formed on the basis of an accommodation of interests or on the basis of an agreement. In either case, the basis of the rational judgment of common interest or of agreement is ultimate value or practical wisdom. A roofer and a plumber might work together as an association because they have practical and clearly defined skills which allow them to work functionally on any project. A communal relationship is one formed on the basis of a subjective feeling by the parties that they belong together, whether the feeling is personal or is linked with tradition. A marriage between two people who are emotionally and sexually attracted to each other could be considered communal because they are willing to face any other conflicts, no matter how serious they might be, in the interest of remaining together. In practice, however, most actual associations and communities incorporate aspects of both types of relationships.

7.3 Social Groups

There are various types of social groups that range from formally structured organizations to those that happen by chance. Sociologists have always been interested in types of social groups and the overall and individual characteristics of their members.

7.3.1 Peer Group

A peer group may be defined as "an association of self-selected equals formed around common interests, sensibilities, preferences, and beliefs." By offering members friendship, a sense of belonging, and acceptance, peer groups compete with the family for the loyalty of their members. Peer groups serve to segregate their members from others on the basis of their age, sex, or generation. A peer group as a type of social group, therefore, consists of those whose ages, interests, and social positions or statuses are relatively equivalent and who are closely associated with one another.

Problem Solving Example:

Q A peer group is defined as "an association of self-selected equals." Which of the following is least likely to be a criterion on which a peer group might segregate its members and why? (1) favorite sports team, (2) taste in music, (3) yearly income, (4) height and weight, (5) church membership.

A Sociologists believe peer groups select their members based on interests, ages, social positions, and statuses that are relatively equivalent. This equality allows the peer group members to challenge one another without the threat that would accompany challenges from family members, especially parents. These groups are formed around common interests, sensibilities, preferences, and beliefs. Peers are influential in individual lifestyle choices—use of alcohol and narcotics, sexual experimentation, and fashion. Of the elements in the question, height and weight are not of themselves indicative of common interests, sensibilities, preferences, or beliefs.

7.3.2 Family

By contrast, the family serves to emotionally bind members of all ages, sexes, and generations. As such, the family is plagued by issues surrounding succession. Particularly in a vacillating period of social change, the conflict between the family and peer group becomes more pronounced, caused by the widening of the cultural gap that separates different generations who may even speak different languages. For example, urbanism (which allowed for sustained contact between age-mates) paved the way not only toward age-grading (the sensitivity toward chronological age gradations characteristic of modern culture), but also toward the age-graded sociability that is characteristic of our times.

7.3.3 Social Groups

Unlike an aggregate, which consists of a number of people who happen to be in the same place at the same time, or a social category, which consists of a number of people with certain characteristics in common, a social group consists of a collection of people interacting with one another in an orderly fashion.

In a social group, there is an interdependence among the various members which forges a feeling of belonging and a sense that the behavior of each person is relevant to the others. Thus, whether or not the membership of a social group is stable or changing, all such group relationships are thought to have two elements in common: (1) members are mutually aware of one another, and (2) members are mutually responsive to one another; therefore, actions are determined by or shaped in the group context.

Social groups have been classified in many different ways—according to the group's size, nature of the interaction, or the kind (quality) of relationship that exists; whether or not membership is voluntary; whether or not a person belongs to and identifies with the group; or according to the group's purpose or composition.

7.3.4 Primary and Secondary Groups

In the early 1920s, sociologist Charles Horton Cooley distinguished between primary groups and secondary groups. In a primary group, the interaction is direct, the common bonds are close and intimate, and the relationships among members are warm, intimate, and personal. In secondary groups, the interaction is anonymous, the bonds are impersonal, the duration of the group is short, and the relationships involve few emotional ties.

Problem Solving Example:

Q Cooley conducted a study of primary and secondary groups. Describe each of these, point out their differences, and give examples of each.

A Members of primary groups have direct, emotional interactions with one another, while members of secondary groups have few emotional ties. Primary groups have close and intimate bonds, they last a long time, and members share norms and values. Examples include spouses, parents and children, and close friends. Secondary group encounters are often anonymous, impersonal interactions that are relatively short in duration. Examples include employers and employees.

7.4 Characteristics of Groups

Through the years, sociologists have developed various theories about groups. The following sections offer a sampling of these theories.

7.4.1 Gemeinschaft and Gesellschaft

Ferdinand Toennies (1887) distinguished between *Gemeinschaft* (community) and *Gesellschaft* (society). By Gemeinschaft, Toennies was referring to small communities characterized by tradition and united by the belief in common ancestry or by geographic proximity.

By Gesellschaft, Toennies was referring to contractual relationships of a voluntary nature, of limited duration and quality, based on rational self-interest, and formed for the explicit purpose of achieving a particular goal.

7.4.2 Dyad and Triad

Focused on discovering the various and relatively stable forms of social relationships where interaction takes place, Georg Simmel (1891) made the distinction between the dyad of two people, in which either member's departure destroys the group, and the triad of three, the addition of a third person sometimes serving as a mediator or nonpartisan party. An example of a triad with a mediator to close the circle is parents who strengthen their mutual love and union by conceiving a child. A nonpartisan-based triad is typified by a mediator who seeks harmony among colliding parties or who, as an arbitrator, seeks to balance competing claims.

7.4.3 Group Size and Other General Structural Properties

Small groups, as the name suggests, have so few members as to allow them to relate as whole persons. The smallest group consists of only two persons. Robert Bales developed the technique of interaction process analysis, that is, a technique of observing and immediately classifying, in predetermined ways, the ongoing activity in small groups.

Also, J. L. Moreno developed the technique of sociometry, a technique focused on establishing the direction of the interactions in small groups. An example of this technique is assessing who is interacting with whom by asking such questions as, "Who is your best friend in the group?" or "With whom would you most like to work on an important project?"

In addition to size, some of the other general structural properties and related social processes that affect the functioning of social groups are (1) the extent of association (for instance, it has been suggested that the more people associate, the more common values and norms they share and the greater the tendency to get along) and (2) the social network of persons that comprises all the relationships in which they are involved and groups to which they belong.

7.4.4 Interaction Processes

Also involved in the interaction processes (the ways role partners agree on goals, negotiate reaching them, and distribute resources) are such factors as:

1. the differentiation between the characteristics of the role structure with task or instrumental roles. Instrumental roles are "oriented" toward specific goals and expressive roles, which are useful in expressing and releasing group tension.

2. front stage (public) and backstage (free of public scrutiny) behavior.

3. principles of exchange (characteristic of market relationships where people bargain for the goods and services they desire).

4. competition between individuals and groups over scarce resources in which the parties not only agree to adhere to certain rules of the game but also believe they are necessary or fair.

5. cooperation (an agreement to share resources for the purpose of achieving a common goal).

6. compromise (an agreement to relinquish certain claims in the interest of achieving more modest goals).

7. conflict (the attempt by one party to destroy, undermine, or harm another) and related methods of reducing or temporarily eliminating conflict, such as coaptation (the case of dissenters being absorbed into the dominant group), mediation (the effort to resolve a conflict through the use of a third party), and the ritualized release of hostility (under carefully controlled circumstances, such as the Olympic games).

7.4.5 In-Group and Out-Group

Other types of social groups include in-groups and out-groups. In-groups are those to which "we" belong. Out-groups are groups toward which one feels a sense of competition or opposition.

7.4.6 Reference Group

Reference groups are social groups that provide the standards by which we evaluate ourselves. For example, if a college student is worried about how her family will react to her grades, she is using her family as a reference group. Similarly, if a lawyer is worried about how the other partners of the firm will react to a recent case he or she lost, the lawyer is using the colleagues as a reference group. These groups can also define the heights and depths of our ambition, such as when we compare ourselves to homeless people or the President of the United States.

7.4.7 Group Conformity and Groupthink

Research on groups has illustrated the power of group pressure to shape human behavior. Group conformity refers to individuals' compliance with group goals, in spite of the fact that group goals may be in conflict with individual goals. In an attempt to be accepted or "fit in," individuals may engage in behaviors they normally would not.

Groupthink, a related phenomenon, occurs when group members begin to think similarly and conform to one another's views. The danger in this is that decisions may be made from a narrow view. Rather than exploring various sides of an issue, group members seeking conformity may adopt a limited view.

Problem Solving Example:

Q Marie was in a staff meeting at her job. Also attending were seven of her co-workers and the supervisor of the department. The supervisor announced that a new project had been forwarded to the department, and all staff members were encouraged to work overtime to ensure that the project was completed on time. Though her co-workers agreed to do it, Marie was also pursuing a degree in sociology, which required that she spend many hours studying after work. Marie wanted to support the department's goals, but she was reluctant to sacrifice her valuable study time. If Marie were to comply with group conformity, what would she do and why?

A In group conformity the individual complies with group goals, even if group goals are in conflict with individual goals, in an effort to be accepted or "fit in." It is likely that Marie would be silent about her concerns, not wishing to threaten her relationship with other group members. She would work the overtime to complete the project. A related phenomenon is groupthink, where group members begin to think similarly and conform to one another's views. If this scenario involved the sharing of opinions on a particular project, Marie would be complying with groupthink if she had strong objections but refrained from voicing her opinion.

7.5   Group Leadership

Leadership is an element of all groups. A leader is a person who initiates the behavior of others by directing, organizing, influencing, or controlling what members do and how they think.

7.5.1   Instrumental and Expressive Leaders

Group research has found two different types of leaders: instrumental (task-oriented leaders who organize the group in the pursuit of its goals) and expressive (social-emotional leaders who achieve harmony and solidarity among group members by offering emotional support).

7.5.2   Authoritarian, Democratic, and Laissez-faire Styles of Leadership

Among the various styles of leadership are the authoritarian leader who gives orders, the democratic leader who seeks a consensus on the course of action to be taken, and the laissez-faire leader who mainly lets the group be—doing little to provide direction or organization.

7.6   Organizations

Sociologists use the term *organization* to represent a specific type of social relationship or arrangement between persons, which is either closed to, or limits the admission of, outsiders. Regulations are enforced by a person(s) in authority, active in enforcing the order governing the organization.

7.6.1 Formal Organizations

A formal organization represents a type of regimented group or structural pattern within which behavior is carried out in a society. It is characterized by (1) formality, (2) a hierarchy of ranked positions, (3) large size, (4) a rather complex division of labor, and (5) continuity beyond its membership.

7.6.2 Informal Organizations

The main focus of an informal organization is to bring people with a common interest together. Once gathered, they are left to openly explore that interest together. A bike club or a bridge club is a good example of an informal organization.

Problem Solving Example:

Q Alfred is studying two organizations for sociology class. The first is the Department of Humanities and Social Sciences at his college. The second is a readers' group that meets monthly at a local bookstore. Are these formal organizations? Why or why not?

A A formal organization is characterized by a high degree of formality, a hierarchy of ranked positions, large size, a rather complex division of labor, and continuity beyond its membership. In general, these organizations are closed to outsiders and regulations are enforced by officials governing the organization. In the above scenario, the Department of Humanities and Social Sciences is clearly a formal organization. The department has a high degree of formality—for example, it relies on records to track students' progress; a hierarchy of ranked positions—lecturers, instructors, professors, etc.; a complex division of labor—administrative and support staff, faculty, and student workers; and continuity beyond its membership—the department continues after students, staff, and faculty leave or retire. The readers' group is not a formal organization: it lacks formality, ranked positions, large size, a complex division of labor, and continuity beyond its members. It is, in short, an informal group.

7.7   Bureaucracy

A bureaucracy is a rationally designed organizational model, the goal of which is to perform complex tasks as efficiently as possible.

7.7.1   Weber's Ideal Type of Bureaucracy

The basic organization of society may be found in its characteristic institution. In prehistoric times, the characteristic institution of most societies was the kin, clan, or sib. In modern times, particularly in the West, as cities became centers for trade and commerce, the characteristic institution became, and remains today, a bureaucracy.

A bureaucracy is a rational system of organization, administration, discipline, and control. Weber's "ideal type" of bureaucracy has the following characteristics:

1. Paid officials who are on fixed salaries, which are their primary source of income.

2. Officials who are accorded certain rights and privileges as a result of making a career out of holding office.

3. Regular salary increases, seniority rights, and promotions upon passing impersonal exams for these offices.

4. Officials who qualify to enter the organization because of their advanced education or vocational training.

5. The rights, responsibilities, obligations, privileges, and work procedures of these officials are rigidly and formally defined by the organization.

6. Officials are responsible for meeting the obligations of the office and for keeping the funds and files of that office separate from their personal ones.

7. Positions within the bureaucracy are organized hierarchically; that is, each level is under the control and supervision of a higher level.

7.7.2 Bureaucracy in Real Life

Weber never intended his ideal type concept of bureaucracy to be confused with reality. Rather, he intended that it be used as a measuring rod against which to measure empirical reality. For example, in their research on bureaucracy, Joseph Bensman and Bernard Rosenberg (1976) learned that most modern bureaucrats are "people pushing" rather than "pencil pushing" types of white-collar employees. The advancement opportunities for these employees are as dependent on how well they are liked, trusted, and personable, as on how they objectively qualify for a position.

Once alert to the cash value (in terms of income-producing opportunities) of having "personality" in an employee society, the official begins to see him- or herself as a commodity to be marketed and packaged like all other merchandise.

Such a self-rationalization, as described by Karl Mannheim (1940), shows a systematic control of impulses as a first step in planning one's course in life. In accordance with personal goals, the official compares his or her other assets, liabilities, and background to what the market will bear as a first step in the research process of determining how personality must be altered to meet the market's fluctuating demand.

Although the standards to which one must conform will vary from one organization to the next, bureaucrats share the inclination to look for external standards upon which to base the organization's interests, activities, and thoughts. Thus, the appearance of a warm and friendly atmosphere offsets the reality of the tensions that exist but cannot be aired in public. As a compromise, occasions are planned where spontaneity and controlled warmth are deemed acceptable.

In these ways, officials never really internalize their roles or parts. They have no commitment to the organization or to one another beyond the formal requirements of their positions. The bureaucrat's all-too-human quest for personal identification (to personally identify with and relate to people in genuine terms) makes true bureaucratic impersonality impossible to achieve.

7.7.3 Parkinson's Law

In this context, we can begin to understand two well-known criticisms of bureaucracy, expressed in Parkinson's Law and in the Peter Principle. Named after its author, C. Northcote Parkinson, Parkinson's Law states that "in any bureaucratic organization, work expands to fill the time available for its completion."

7.7.4 The Peter Principle

Named after Lawrence Peter, the Peter Principle states that "in any hierarchy, every employee tends to rise to his level of incompetence."

7.7.5 Michels' Iron Law of Oligarchy

We can now also begin to understand the context within which Robert Michels (1915) formulated his famous Iron Law of Oligarchy. As observed by Bensman and Rosenberg, the speedy proliferation of bureaucracy "is connected with everything else that gives our culture its uniqueness," i.e., a money economy, machine production, and the creation of nation-states with large-scale bureaucratic armies.

Bureaucracy also spreads throughout the various branches of civil government following the widening of the political boundaries of territory under the control of a single person. When workers organized for the purpose of protecting and advancing their claims to having certain inalienable rights (whether to form trade unions or political parties), their leadership was bureaucratized.

Thus, Robert Michels had in mind the working-class movements in America and Europe when he designed the Iron Law of Oligarchy, claiming that a small number of specialists generally hold sway over any organization.

Problem Solving Examples:

 Describe the characteristics found in a bureaucracy as they relate to the worker in the organization.

A Several characteristics mark the relation of the worker to his or her organization. Bureaucracies are large and have paid officials who have certain rights and privileges that accompany their positions. Hiring and promoting are based on formal examinations or evaluations. Bureaucracies have a hierarchical organization with lower- ranking officials supervised by higher-ranking officials. They are governed by rules and regulations that pertain to all operations, and they maintain records of transactions. Some clear examples of bureaucracies are government agencies, large private foundations, and corporations. (See Weber, *Economy and Society*, 1922.)

Quiz: Groups and Organizations

1. The ways in which role partners agree on goals, negotiate reaching them, and distribute resources are called _____ processes.

    (A) network

    (B) interaction

    (C) social

    (D) power

    (E) domination

2. The proposition that in any bureaucratic organization "work expands to fill the time available for its completion" is a statement of

    (A) Robert's Rule.

    (B) the Peter Principle.

    (C) the Iron Law of Oligarchy.

    (D) Weber's Ideal Type.

    (E) Parkinson's Law.

3. An assembly of people united through interaction is referred to as a

   (A) crowd.

   (B) mob.

   (C) social network.

   (D) social group.

   (E) social club.

4. Task-oriented leaders who organize the group in pursuit of goals are _____ leaders.

   (A) autocratic

   (B) ineffective

   (C) charismatic

   (D) traditional

   (E) instrumental

5. Weber's concept of _____ was not a representation of reality, but a rod with which to measure empirical reality.

   (A) Verstehen

   (B) Protestant ethic

   (C) the ideal type

   (D) formal organization

   (E) None of the above.

6. Social-emotional leaders who achieve harmony and solidarity among group members are _____ leaders.

   (A) repressive

   (B) expressive

   (C) autocratic

(D) traditional

(E) None of the above.

7. The principle that in any hierarchy every employee tends to rise to his or her level of incompetence has been attributed to _____, after whom this principle has been named.

(A) Max Weber

(B) C. Northcote Parkinson

(C) Robert Michels

(D) Lawrence Peter

(E) Karl Mannheim

8. An _____ is a relationship formed on the basis of accommodation of interests or on the basis of an agreement. In comparison, a _____ relationship is based on subjective feelings that the members "belong together."

(A) association, communal

(B) association, secondary

(C) association, casual

(D) association, professional

(E) None of the above.

9. Georg Simmel investigated two simple forms of social interaction, the _____, in which the removing of one member destroys the group, and the _____, in which a third person is introduced as a mediator or third party.

(A) in-group, out-group

(B) Gemeinschaft, Gesellschaft

(C) dyad, triad

(D) primary, secondary

(E) secondary, primary

10. Unlike peer groups, _____ tend to bind members of all ages, sexes, and various generations.

    (A) aggregates

    (B) dyads

    (C) reference groups

    (D) families

    (E) All of the above.

ANSWER KEY

1.	(B)	6.	(B)
2.	(E)	7.	(D)
3.	(D)	8.	(A)
4.	(E)	9.	(C)
5.	(C)	10.	(D)

CHAPTER 8

Deviance

8.1 Defining Deviance

Strictly speaking, deviance represents a departure from a norm. Although deviance is usually associated with criminal activity or mental illness, it also includes behavior that stands out as being more ambitious, industrious, heroic, or righteous than the rest—behavior that is generally neither expected nor very frequently found. It includes behavior that is not thought to be particularly significant even though it represents a violation of a norm.

However, sociologists have concerned themselves with deviant behavior that violates, or is contrary to, the rules of acceptable and appropriate behavior of a group or society. This perception by the group becomes evident in the strong negative reaction, or ridicule, generated by the members of the group.

Sociologists have tended to differ in their understanding of deviance. The question is whether or not deviance represents more than a violation of a norm and, if so, what this contrary behavior is thought ultimately to represent.

8.2 Deviance and Stigma

Consistent with an orientation toward society as a whole, the one characteristic shared by those with deviant reputations is stigma. A stigma is the mark of social disgrace that sets the deviant apart from other members of society who regard themselves as "normal." In most instances, people escape having their deviant behavior discovered. Because they are not stigmatized or marked as deviant, they think of themselves as being relatively normal.

Deviance is seen as relative to the time, place, and context of a group or society in which it is observed. In addition, it is also relative to the social status of the person defining the behavior, and to whether or not that person is in a position to label the behavior as "deviant."

Problem Solving Example:

 Deviant behavior is transferable from society to society. Offer a challenge to this statement.

Sociologists contend that deviance is relative to the time, place, and context of a group or society in which it is observed. For example, being nude in public is considered deviant behavior in American society, but in some European cultures public nudity—on the performance stage or on the beach—is not considered deviant. Additionally, during the Victorian era, even in Europe, public nudity of any variety and in any location would have been considered deviant. Whether or not a behavior is deviant is also relative to the social status of the person engaging in the behavior. For example, the wearing of an earring by men of high social status—corporate presidents or members of Congress—might be considered inappropriate (deviant), but the same judgment is not likely to be made of an artist or musical performer. Sociologists have not agreed in their understanding of deviance or what it represents in society.

8.3 Deviance, Conformity, Social Order, and Social Control

Even if most people have violated significant social norms at some point in their lives, the majority of people at any given moment are thought to be conforming to those norms that are important to a society's continued existence. It is because of this that social order exists.

It is believed that a social order depends on its members generally knowing and doing what is expected of them. They have common values and guidelines to which they generally adhere. These norms prescribe the behavior that is appropriate to a situation as it is given or commonly construed at the time. In other words, a social order presumably cannot exist without an effective system of social control. Social control is best defined as a series of measures that serve as a general guarantee of people conforming to norms, i.e., doing what's expected and appropriate. These measures may include punishment for inappropriate behavior, such as arrest by formal authorities or expulsion from a social group.

Through the process of socialization, social control is achieved. The success of this is demonstrated by the fact that most people usually do what is expected out of sheer habit and without question. When socialization cannot guarantee sufficient conformity through the informal, as well as the formal and organized, ways of rewarding conformity and punishing nonconformity, there comes a need for negative sanctions. Negative sanctions indicate that social control has failed and that deviance has occurred.

Deviance represents a residual category of behavior unlike that which is generally found. This behavior, unless adequately checked, may threaten the effectiveness of the system of social control and the social order. Ultimately, some deviance is necessary so that the boundaries of permissible behavior may be defined. The major function of deviance is to reassure people that the system of social control is working effectively.

Problem Solving Example:

Q Sociologists believe that social control guarantees that people will conform to social norms. Social norms prescribe the behavior that is appropriate to a situation as it is given or commonly construed at the time. How is social control achieved?

A Socialization ensures that most people do what is expected by applying rewards and punishments for conformity and nonconformity, respectively. Society's survival depends on most people doing what is expected. Most members of social groups do what is expected out of habit, without question. This behavior results from the use of formal and informal social control mechanisms. Informal mechanisms include spontaneous expressions of approval or disapproval from social agents—for example, family or peers. Formal mechanisms include law enforcement agents who are charged with enforcing social norms.

8.4 Deviance and Social Groups

Deviance represents an unusual departure from an established group rule of acceptable conduct. These rules denote a negotiated world of meanings; they shape what individuals perceive and how they behave, thereby eliminating the uncertainty that exists in the absence of such guidelines. Calling attention to a departure from the rules assures members that they are "normal." Members can feel that their own behavior falls within the usual limits of what is and what is not acceptable in the group, while ridiculing those whose observed behavior departs from the expected.

In this way, the social order, which depends upon people doing what others expect of them, is more or less guaranteed. Those who usually behave in socially approved ways are provided with a reason for continuing to do what is expected. Those who have departed from the rules have a reason to avoid behaving in ways that are unacceptable to group members.

Given the many different groups that make up a society, and the competing values and range of interests they represent, social order is never guaranteed or certain without a value system. Value systems enjoy such wide acceptance in society that even those groups that represent opposing interests find them to be consistent with, or suited to, their own concerns.

In the competition or struggle between groups, those with the most to lose or gain, or those who feel most strongly about their causes, may succeed in defining and shaping the standards of right and wrong that become the group's norms. But, they may never succeed in altering the meaning that represents the core values or culture of a society.

Both conforming and deviant behaviors are socially constructed relative to the culture of the society in which they occur. Sometimes "deviant" actions are those that powerful people, those in a position to both define and enforce social norms, find threatening. Because this sector of society agrees with, supports, and serves to define the status quo, anything that threatens this sector is then labeled deviant. In this way, deviance is defined by its opposite rather than any inherent threat it may pose.

Particularly in complex societies, some norms are thought to be more important than others in that they involve behavior necessary for a group's continuity, survival, or well-being. This is evidenced by the severity of the sanctions associated with them. Whether or not norms are proscriptive ("thou shalt not") or prescriptive ("thou shalt"), their definitions change over time and from one society to the next, but never so much as to be inconsistent with a society's core values.

8.5 Functions and Deviance

In terms of the group, deviance serves several functions. According to Durkheim's viewpoint, deviance serves to unify the group by identifying the limits of acceptable behavior and, thus, showing who are insiders and who are outsiders. Deviance also serves as a safety valve that allows people to express discontent with existing norms without threatening the social order. Principled challenges to norms are possible.

Social control refers to the ways of getting people to conform to norms. Such techniques, which include persuasion, teaching, and force, may be planned or unplanned, may be informal (involving the approval or disapproval of significant others) or formal (involving those in positions responsible for enforcing norms). In this context, primary deviance is the term used to refer to behavior violating a norm, while secondary deviance refers to the behavior that results from the social response to such deviance.

For example: A teenager who tries drugs is engaging in primary deviance. In response to this behavior, he may be arrested and/or severely censured in some way. This may leave him without friends or with a general sense of resentment toward mainstream society. In response to this treatment, he may join a street gang where he may engage in behaviors that are deliberately destructive to the society that has cast him out (secondary deviance).

It is in connection with secondary deviance that stigma symbolizes a moral blemish or undesirable label that tends to be extended to other undesirable traits. Deviant subcultures represent peer groups that support deviance by providing social networks to deviants.

Problem Solving Example:

 Some sociologists contend that deviance serves an important function in society. What is the function?

Social groups are unified by deviance, in that they identify the limits of acceptable behavior and mark (or label) insiders and outsiders. Durkheim, for instance, concluded that deviance also allows group members to express discontent with existing norms without threatening social order. That is, by identifying deviant behavior, the group records what is unacceptable behavior in its members, allowing a member who wants to demonstrate discontent with norms to step outside of approved behavior. For example, women protesting for equal rights might burn their bras, or gay men and lesbians might parade in the streets holding hands with and kissing other members of the same sex. In this way, the protesting women and gay men and lesbians hope to push the boundaries of social acceptance to promote social change. Ironically, it can be argued that these actions confirm societal norms among the majority of group members and sustain the traditional order.

8.6　Biological Explanations of Deviance

In 1875 Cesare Lombroso published the results of his studies comparing the body measurements of institutionalized criminals, noncriminals, and "primitive" human beings. He concluded that deviant behavior is inherited and that the body measurements of criminals bore a greater resemblance to apes than to noncriminals.

William Sheldon (1941) based his work on the earlier work of Ernst Kretschmer (1925). He classified people according to their body types. He concluded that a relationship exists between body type, psychological state, and criminal behavior (with endomorphs, being soft and fat, and prone to manic depression and alcoholism; ectomorphs, being lean and thin, and prone to schizophrenia; and the muscular and large-boned, or mesomorphs, being prone to criminal behavior, alcoholism, and manic depression).

Studies attempting to link criminal behavior and body type have not always produced consistent results. More recently, efforts have been made to link deviant behavior with an "abnormal" (XYY) chromosomal pattern found among inmates of prisons and mental hospitals. This pattern is unlike the usual male XY pattern or female XX pattern. Researchers also have been studying the relationship between the brain, body chemistry, diet, and behavior.

Problem Solving Example:

Q In searching for answers to criminal behavior, some early scientists theorized that there was a relationship between body type and criminal behavior. Describe the three body types and their associated behaviors.

A William Sheldon classified all people according to the three body types: endomorph, ectomorph, and mesomorph. Sheldon contended that muscular and large-boned mesomorphs were more prone to alcoholism and manic depression, as well as criminal behavior. Endomorphs, those with short and fat bodies, were also believed to be more inclined to manic depression and alcoholism. Ectomorphs, the small and thin, were believed to be prone to schizophrenia. Scientists have also looked for chromosomal links to deviant behavior (e.g., the presence of XYY chromosome patterns among prison inmates and patients in mental hospitals). The usual male pattern is XY and the female pattern is XX. Sociologists have been most concerned with the deviant behaviors and their social contexts, not with the biological or psychological sources of these behaviors and actions.

8.7 Psychological Explanations of Deviance

Psychologists have attributed antisocial or deviant behavior to the unconscious, making itself known to a superego that lacks the strength to overcome the id. This way of thinking was influenced by Freud and others who sought to trace personality and behavior to early childhood learning experiences and the manner in which the repression of the powerful biological drives of the id takes place. The unconscious is that part of the mind where unpleasant, or perhaps even antisocial, memories of experience are stored.

Such research has supported the use of personality tests to identify troublemakers and delinquents, to assess the guilt or innocence of those suspected of committing a crime, and to ferret out problems before they occur.

8.8 Sociological Explanations of Deviance

Sociological explanations of deviance fall into two categories. The first category includes those sociologists who assume that most people conform most of the time as a consequence of adequate socialization. They treat deviance as a special category of behavior and the deviant as deserving of special consideration. They ask why every society has known deviance. They want to know why people become deviant. They wonder why social control mechanisms are applied as a means of limiting and punishing clear violations of significant social norms.

The second category includes those sociologists who tend to locate the source of deviance outside the individual person. They look within the social structure or to a social process of labeling. Labeling focuses on the process through which persons come to be defined as deviant. It also focuses on the means through which deviant behavior is created by the interaction taking place between those committing acts in violation of group norms and those responding to such violations.

Durkheim understood deviance to be a product of the structural circumstance of disorganization, confusion, or anomie both in society and in the individual, resulting from weak, conflicting, or nonexistent norms. To expand on this, Robert Merton (1957) pointed to situations in which there is a disjunction between means and ends. For example, such a disjunction occurs in American society's placing an emphasis on wealth and success, while not offering those in less powerful positions legitimate opportunities to achieve them. People seek to fill this gap in a number of ways:

- The "conformists" seek to continue the acceptance of the goals and means offered for their attainment.

- The "innovators" may continue to accept the goals while seeking new, and in many cases, illegitimate, revenues for the attainment of these goals.

- The "ritualists" may make the means into an end by rejecting the culturally prescribed goals as being out of their reach. These people are in favor of an overemphasis upon the means of achieving these goals. An example of this would be the bureaucrat who is more concerned with adhering to the rules and with keeping his job than with his own personal achievement.

- The "retreats" reject both the means and ends offered by society and adopt new standards of living, such as dropping into drug use, mental illness, alcoholism, homelessness, etc.

- The "rebellious" reject both the means and ends while seeking to replace both with alternatives, thereby changing the way society as a whole is structured.

In his theory of differential association, Edwin Sutherland (1939) concluded that criminal behavior is learned through social interaction in primary groups. His theory states that it is in the primary group that a person acquires knowledge of the techniques used in committing crimes. This primary group also provides reasons for conforming to or violating rules of permissive or nonpermissive behavior in a given situation, as well as an understanding of what motivates criminal activity. It is claimed that becoming a criminal means that the benefits favorably outweigh the disadvantages of violating the law. Moreover, the kinds of differential associations favoring criminal activity occur frequently, are long-lasting and intense, and take place earlier rather than later in life.

Problem Solving Examples:

Q Joe lives in a poor urban neighborhood. He has sought opportunities to escape the poverty that surrounds him by applying for employment through various agencies. He has been unable to obtain gainful employment because he does not have an automobile. What might Joe's response be, in terms of Robert Merton's theory of individual adaptation to cultural means and goals?

A Because the innovator accepts society's goals while seeking new and often illegitimate means to attain these goals, Joe might steal an automobile so that he can get legitimate employment. He might also turn to drug dealing or numbers running. According to Merton, other possible responses include: a conformist response, in which Joe would strive to attain his goal through legitimate means, such as taking a part-time job to save up for a car; a ritualist response, in which he would continue to work with no thought of achieving the desired goals, focusing on the work instead, because the goals are out of reach; a retreat, in which Joe would drop out of society completely and fall into drug abuse, alcoholism, or mental illness; and a rebellious response, in which he would seek to change the social system completely, for example, through political or religious radicalism.

Q Harold has been arrested for holding up a downtown convenience store. Harold comes from an impoverished inner-city background. He has been a member of a gang since he was 12. This is his third offense and he will likely be sentenced to 20 years in prison. Sociologists Robert Merton and Edwin Sutherland offer two different theories of criminal behavior. How might Merton and Sutherland explain Harold's descent into crime?

A Merton might classify Harold's behavior as the "innovation" model of adapting to cultural means and goals. He might argue that Harold seeks the wealth and success that are promoted by society, but he has sought an illegitimate means of acquiring society's goals. On the other hand, Sutherland might argue it is in the primary group that a person learns the techniques used to commit crimes and where he/she is given reasons for conforming to or violating rules. Sutherland might argue that Harold had frequent associations that favored criminal activity. These associations were long lasting, intense, and occurred early in life.

Quiz: Deviance

1. The mind sometimes stores unpleasant and perhaps antisocial memories of experiences in the

   (A) id.

   (B) ego.

   (C) genes.

   (D) unconscious.

   (E) personality.

2. A mark of social disgrace, or _____, sets the deviant apart from other members of society.

   (A) tattoo

   (B) brand

   (C) stigma

   (D) demerit

   (E) curse

3. Sociologists refer to any violation of the law as

   (A) a felony.

   (B) a deviant act.

   (C) juvenile delinquency.

   (D) white-collar crime.

   (E) crime.

4. Regarding theories of deviance, the idea that an individual commits deviant acts because he or she "hangs out" with the wrong crowd follows what line of thinking?

   (A) Differential association

   (B) Strain theory

   (C) Labeling theory

   (D) Control theory

   (E) None of the above.

5. Which sociologist's explanation of deviant behavior most clearly reflects the perspective of functionalist theory, arguing that deviance is precipitated by contradictions or inconsistencies in the social system?

   (A) Charles H. Cooley

   (B) Edwin Lemert

   (C) Edwin Sutherland

   (D) Robert K. Merton

   (E) Thomas Scheff

6. Deviance can help clarify social norms, increase group cohesion of those who conform, and can provide employment for those dealing with deviance. These are social benefits of deviance associated most closely with the _____ viewpoint on deviance.

   (A) functionalist

   (B) conflict

   (C) symbolic interactionist

   (D) interpretative

   (E) None of the above.

7. Deviant behavior is the term used by sociologists to describe behaviors that a group defines as

    (A) violating basic norms.

    (B) uncommonly brave or heroic.

    (C) the standard for others to follow.

    (D) very rare or unusual.

    (E) based on personal motives.

8. Which of the following behaviors would NOT be considered an example of deviance in contemporary American society?

    (A) Eating spaghetti with one's fingers

    (B) Running naked down a busy city street

    (C) A man regularly dressing in women's clothing

    (D) College students drinking beer on a Saturday night

    (E) A person talking to himself in public places

9. Which of the following is NOT a method of social control?

    (A) Ridicule

    (B) Insults

    (C) Spanking

    (D) Praise

    (E) Imitation

10. A biological theory of crime, which maintains that the criminal inherits his or her propensities toward crime, represents a genetic throwback to early humans and may be identified visually by certain physical features best describes

    (A) Howard Becker's labeling theory.

    (B) Cesare Lombroso's atavistic theory.

    (C) the control theory.

(D)   the theory of differential association.

(E)   the XYY chromosome theory.

ANSWER KEY

1.	(D)	6.	(A)
2.	(C)	7.	(A)
3.	(E)	8.	(D)
4.	(A)	9.	(E)
5.	(D)	10.	(B)

CHAPTER 9

Family and Society

9.1 Social Institutions

Social institutions, including family, government, and religion, are organized patterns of beliefs and behaviors focused on meeting society's basic needs. The family is a social creation that transcends the biological basis of its existence. As a unit of organization, it is of particular interest to sociologists.

9.2 Kinship

Kinship is the introduction of symbolic meaning or value to actual or imagined blood ties. Although the biological phenomenon of unity based on reproducing and protecting animal offspring predates man, kinship is a specifically human, intellectual creation. Max Weber found it possible to establish the social origins of kinship by means of cross-cultural comparisons.

In the universal history of culture and as a medium of biological inheritance, the family has been an institutional ally as well as an institutional enemy of the state. Through the family, we can distinguish legitimate from illegitimate offspring, as well as social inheritance.

The concept of social inheritance is the inheritance of the parents' ascribed statuses, as well as any products of their achieved statuses (i.e., wealth, prestige, and power), by the children. It has been the focus of ideological warfare between church and state, and it has been an agency for socialization as well as of oppression.

Problem Solving Example:

Q Gerald is interested in comparing the patterns of kinship of residents of a rural town in the Midwest with those of domesticated livestock in the same region. What is the biggest challenge to Gerald's study?

A Sociologists define kinship as the introduction of symbolic meaning or value to actual or imagined blood ties. Kinship is a specifically human creation. Since the concept is applied only to humans, it would be impossible to gather data from nonhuman subjects.

9.3 Marriage

The social institution of marriage consists of a long-term cooperative relationship—typically between two people—which usually includes sexual intimacy between the partners, but virtually always requires economic cooperation and codependency. Additionally, this union is acknowledged, defined, and often facilitated by the legal institution that regulates behavioral boundaries in society. The legal institution also tends to set the terms under which the individual partners in marriage can have their differences arbitrated.

9.4 Family

The social institution of family is found in every society and is defined as a social group consisting of two or more people related by marriage, through parentage, as siblings, through adoption, or possibly by more distant kinship, such as cousins, nieces, nephews, etc. The more distant the kinship relationship, the more arbitrary the ascribed familial identification. Each culture may have very different limits at which that identification dissolves. The more distant the kinship, the more that identification is subject to individual cultural definitions.

9.4.1 Types of Families

The idea of family can be broadly broken down into four components. The family of orientation is the unit into which a person is born. The family of procreation is the unit, usually occurring in adulthood, in which people are able to form social groups of their own through procreation or adoption. The nuclear family consists of people of the opposite sex who are in a socially approved sexual union and living with their children. The extended family is one in which the notion of consanguinity has been extended beyond the immediate (nuclear) family to those families who are indirectly linked by blood.

9.5 Forms of Vested Authority

Authority can be vested in either the father or the mother of a family. When the father has vested authority, the family is referred to as a patriarchy. When the mother has vested authority, the family is referred to as a matriarchy.

The terms "patrilineal" and "matrilineal" indicate where descent may be traced (through the father or mother).

9.6 Endogamy and Exogamy: Marriage Patterns

Most societies practice endogamy (marriage within certain specific groups) or exogamy (marriage outside certain specific groups). In the United States, for instance, marriage within one's immediate family is not permitted; one must marry an outsider. This is known as exogamy.

By contrast, interracial marriages are often discouraged. Hence, social pressure exists to avoid marrying someone of a different race, thus discouraging exogamy.

Marriage between members of the same religious faith is sometimes encouraged. There is sometimes great social pressure to marry someone of the same religious faith, or to practice endogamy.

9.7 Monogamy and Polygamy: Marriage Patterns

Monogamy means having one spouse at a time. Serial monogamy, which involves marriage, and divorce, followed by remarriage, has become less of the exception and more the rule in America.

Polygamy means having more than one spouse at a time. Three types of polygamy are known to exist. The first is polygyny, which refers to the practice of a man having several wives at once. The second is polyandry, which refers to the practice of a woman having several husbands at once. The third type is group marriage, which refers to a marriage between two or more men and two or more women.

9.8 Residential Patterns: Patrilocality, Matrilocality, and Neolocality

Patrilocality, matrilocality, and neolocality indicate where newly-weds customarily reside. Patrilocality occurs when the newlyweds reside with the husband's extended family; matrilocality occurs when they reside with the wife's extended family; neolocality occurs when they live in a new or separate residence.

Because there is no necessary correlation between power, descent, and residence, patriarchies may be matrilineal or matrilocal, they may include the levirate (which obliges a man to marry his brother's widow or suffer disgrace), or they may permit the transmission of property to the eldest son, a practice called primogeniture, or to the youngest son, which is called ultimogeniture.

Problem Solving Example:

Q Henry is a 33-year-old African American and Alice is an 18-year-old Asian American. They have made plans to marry and live abroad, over the objections of their parents, who prefer endogamous marriages. Why would theirs not be an endogamous marriage?

A The practice of endogamy describes marriage within certain specific groups. Often these groups are racial or ethnic. Since Henry and Alice do not belong to the same ethnic group, their marriage would be exogamous. Exogamy is the practice of marrying outside one's group. Age is not a factor in endogamy, so the 15-year difference in their ages is not the focus of concern, and neither is where the couple will live. However, some cultures do have customs surrounding where the couple resides. If Henry and Alice were to live with either his or her family, they would be patrilocal or matrilocal, respectively. Since they plan to move away from both families, they will be neolocal.

Quiz: Family and Society

1. The concept of social inheritance involves the inheritance of _____ status, as well as wealth, prestige, and power.

    (A) primary and secondary

    (B) biological and psychological

    (C) general and specific

    (D) relative and absolute

    (E) ascribed

2. _____ found it possible to establish the social origins of kinship by means of cross-cultural comparisons.

    (A) William Sheldon

    (B) Jean Piaget

    (C) Emile Durkheim

    (D) Max Weber

    (E) Robert Merton

3. Since getting married and having a child, Mary has two families. Her parents are her family of _____ and her spouse and child are her family of _____.

    (A) procreation, orientation

    (B) procreation, adoption

    (C) orientation, procreation

    (D) orientation, cooperation

    (E) orientation, adoption

4. Mr. and Mrs. Desai Singh live with their two sons, Rabindranath and Krishna, and their wives, Namitha and Anitra, respectively, and their seven children (Mr. and Mrs. Singh's grandchildren) in what is known as

    (A) a serially monogamous family.

    (B) an extended family.

    (C) a nuclear family.

    (D) a dysfunctional family.

    (E) a polygamous family.

5. Which of the following terms would be an accurate description of family and kinship practices that are most prominent in the United States today?

    I.   Matrilineal descent system

    II. Nuclear family

    III. Neolocal family

    IV. Matriarchal family

    (A) I only.

    (B) I and II only.

    (C) I, II, and III only.

(D) I and III only.

(E) II and III only.

6. The belief that men are superior and should be in control in the family and in society is called

(A) patriarchy.

(B) matriarchy.

(C) patrilineal.

(D) patrilocal.

(E) paternal.

7. Jose and Maria met, fell in love, and decided to marry. They are both Catholic and of Puerto Rican ancestry. Their marriage illustrates which of the following?

(A) The norm of exogamy

(B) The norm of endogamy

(C) Arranged marriages

(D) The stimulus-value-role theory

(E) Polyandrous marriages

8. Lorraine and Bob get married and move near the bride's parents. The phrase that best describes this situation is

(A) matrilocal residence.

(B) patrilocal residence.

(C) matrilineal.

(D) monogamy.

(E) polygamy.

9. When a society has a norm that permits a man to have more than one wife at the same time, this is called the norm of

    (A) monogamy.

    (B) serial monogamy.

    (C) group marriage.

    (D) polygyny.

    (E) polyandry.

10. Bob Jones has two children, Sara and Arthur. Both of them share his family name, Jones. When they start families of their own, Arthur's children will be named Jones, but Sarah's children will take the name of their father. This family uses a _____ system to trace descent.

    (A) patriotic

    (B) patrilocal

    (C) patrilineal

    (D) patronizing

    (E) patriarchal

ANSWER KEY

1.	(E)	6.	(A)
2.	(D)	7.	(B)
3.	(C)	8.	(A)
4.	(B)	9.	(D)
5.	(E)	10.	(C)

CHAPTER 10

Economics and Society

10.1 Traditionalism and Economic Rationality

From the standpoint of society as a whole, the economic order is the institutionalized organizational system of norms and behavioral patterns through which goods and services are produced, distributed, and consumed. By definition, economic life includes the work we do, what type of economic organization we belong to, why we do it, and the measure of success attained as shown by wealth, property, income, and the occupation itself.

In this context, traditionalism represents the type of economic motivation that sanctifies the past by preserving a certain practice because it has always been that way. Its opposite, economic rationality, represents the type of economic motivation that embraces change and development, such as in the methods of production. Economic rationality sanctifies progress and emphasizes practicality, with profits being "the touchstone of economic efficiency."

In the past, guild masters monopolized their positions of power based on heredity and created a class of workers who had no chance of becoming masters themselves. Changes were brought about in the methods of production and the rules governing how much capital equipment a guild master could own, and how many journeymen he could employ. These economic changes brought about the crystallization of the class comprised of capitalists and workers known as the "working class."

10.2 Division of Labor

The division of labor is the manner in which work is divided among individuals and groups specialized in particular economic activities.

10.3 Comparative Economic Systems

Capitalism represents one type of economic system in which there is private ownership of the means of producing and distributing goods and services. The most widely used example of a capitalist society is the United States.

Socialism represents another type of economic system in which there is public ownership of the means of producing and distributing goods and services. Actual economic systems, however, are more often a blend of capitalist and socialist elements today. The former Soviet Union possessed an economy based on socialism.

Problem Solving Example:

Q Harry is studying the economic systems of developing countries. He has begun his study by categorizing the systems as capitalism-based or socialism-based. What criteria might Harry use to determine which countries fit which categories? Describe the essential difference between capitalism-based and socialism-based systems.

A Harry must examine each country's norms and practices in relation to the production, distribution, and consumption of goods and services. The capitalist, free-enterprise system features primarily private ownership or control of production. The socialist system features public ownership of the means of production and distribution. Sociologists have found that most economic systems are actually a blend of capitalist and socialist systems. For example, in Sweden and Denmark, production is privately owned, but the distribution of goods and services is centrally controlled.

10.4 Sectors of the Economy

The primary, secondary, and tertiary sectors of an economy involve different ways of producing goods and services and selling them for a profit.

10.4.1 Primary Sector

The primary sector is involved in the extraction of raw materials and natural resources. Primary production then consists of activities such as hunting, gathering, farming, and mining, in which people are directly involved with the extraction and cultivation of natural resources.

10.4.2 Secondary Sector

The secondary sector is involved in turning raw materials acquired through primary production into the manufactured goods we use, such as furniture, cars, and homes. Secondary production consists of the techniques and activities involved in manufacturing goods, i.e., in making items such as pottery, bows and arrows, cards, and nuclear weaponry.

10.4.3 Tertiary Sector

The tertiary (or service) sector is involved in providing services in areas such as health, education, welfare, and entertainment. Tertiary production consists of the kinds of assistance or service that people offer, such as baby-sitting, plumbing, keyboarding, teaching, and nursing.

Problem Solving Example:

Q This list of occupations—tailor, coal miner, autoworker— corresponds to the various sectors of a capitalist economy. What are those sectors, in the order they are listed above?

A They are tertiary, primary, and secondary. The tertiary sector provides services to consumers—barbers, tailors, and house-keepers. The primary sector is involved in the extraction of raw materials—miners and lumberjacks. The secondary sector turns the raw materials into manufactured goods—automobile and textile factory workers. These three sectors are often linked so that a product passes through all stages before reaching the end consumer. The tailor creates a jacket (tertiary) from cloth woven at a textile mill (secondary) with wool sheared by a sheep rancher (primary).

10.5 Distribution Systems

There are various types of distribution systems, including the barter system and the free-market system. The barter system consists of the direct exchange of goods or services for other goods or services judged to be of equivalent value. Prior to the use of money as a medium of trade, individuals bartered. For example, a woman who needs a house built may exchange some of her land for the wood necessary to build the house.

The free-market system of exchanging goods and services is one in which value is determined by supply and demand.

Quiz: Economics and Society

1. Most economic systems in the world may be classified as

    (A) capitalist.

    (B) socialist.

    (C) mixed economies.

    (D) laissez-faire economies.

    (E) communist economies.

2. In order to support her family, Mary works as a truck driver and is a member of the Teamsters Union. These are all aspects of

    (A) economic life.

    (B) economic organization.

(C)   economic order.

(D)   economic motivation.

(E)   economic efficiency.

3.   Giant Motor Corporation in Detroit produces sports cars. Rather than supply their own raw materials, they have contracted the Forge Mining Company to supply their steel. They also buy their electronic parts from another small company and have their engines assembled in New Jersey. This practice is known as

(A)   bureaucracy.

(B)   division of labor.

(C)   economic organization.

(D)   economic distribution.

(E)   capitalism.

4.   Goods are manufactured by which sector of the economy?

(A)   Foreign workers

(B)   Laborers

(C)   The tertiary sector

(D)   The secondary sector

(E)   Mills

5.   The type of economic motivation that embraces change and development is called

(A)   economic progressivism.

(B)   economic radicalism.

(C)   economic rationality.

(D)   economic stimulation.

(E)   economic structuralism.

6. The economic system that features public ownership of the means of producing and distributing goods and services is called

    (A) pauperism.

    (B) socialism.

    (C) liberalism.

    (D) democracy.

    (E) None of the above.

7. The exchange of goods or services for others judged to be of equal value is called

    (A) economics.

    (B) haggling.

    (C) capitalism.

    (D) bartering.

    (E) bonding.

8. The type of economic motivation that sanctifies the past by preserving a certain practice because it has always been that way is called

    (A) economic provincialism.

    (B) economic adventurism.

    (C) economic progressivism.

    (D) economic traditionalism.

    (E) None of the above.

9. The primary sector is involved with the extraction and cultivation of

    (A) raw materials.

    (B) currency.

    (C) labor.

(D) intellect.

(E) None of the above.

10. The tertiary sector workers are involved in health care, education, and welfare industries. They are often called _____ workers.

(A) minimum-wage

(B) service

(C) servile

(D) nonessential

(E) temporary

ANSWER KEY

1. (C)   6. (B)
2. (A)   7. (D)
3. (B)   8. (D)
4. (D)   9. (A)
5. (C)   10. (B)

CHAPTER 11

Politics and Society

11.1 The Political Order

From the standpoint of society as a whole, the political order is the institutionalized system of organizational and behavioral patterns through which power is legitimately acquired and exercised.

As understood by Max Weber, a belief in legitimacy, the right of those in positions of power to command, is fundamental to all forms of authority. Without the consent of the governed, the state's monopoly on the legitimate use of force is more than likely to be questioned.

11.2 Three Types of Authority

Max Weber differentiated between three types of authority: traditional, rational-legal, and charismatic. He divided them according to how the right or power to command and the duty to obey are interpreted. Traditional authority is based on long-held and sacred customs. Rational-legal authority stems from within the framework of a body of laws that have been duly enacted. Charismatic authority is based on the extraordinary, uncanny, and supernatural powers or abilities that have been associated with a particular person.

Thus, in pre-industrial times, traditional authority, the power generated by respect for long-held norms, dominated. As societies industrialized, however, the importance of traditional authority declined. Charismatic authority exists when power is legitimated through the unique, extraordinary, personal abilities of an individual. Individual leaders who are seen by the public as magnetic and forceful are granted power. Typically, rational-legal authority, which is legally circumscribed by rules and regulations, is found within modern formal organizations.

Problem Solving Example:

Q George has been studying the development of leaders among street gangs in his city. George has noticed that leadership roles are based on the charismatic type of authority. What is the charismatic type of authority?

A Charismatic authority exists when power is granted by followers in recognition of the unique, extraordinary, personal abilities of an individual. Sociologists have often cited Lenin, Hitler, and Roosevelt as three very different political leaders, each with substantial charismatic authority—whose followers were generally willing to follow without question. Max Weber identified two other types of authority: rational-legal authority based on duly enacted laws—for example, democratically elected presidents—and traditional authority based on long-held or sacred customs—for example, fathers as the patriarchal heads of households. (See Weber, *Economy and Society*, 1922.)

11.3 Types of Government

Forms of government depend upon the types of relationships that exist between the ruler and the ruled. Three types of government are as follows: authoritarian, totalitarian, and democratic.

11.3.1 Authoritarian

An authoritarian form of government is one in which rulers tolerate little, if any, opposition to their authority. Such governments deny popular participation in decision making. Individuals have little or no voice in government operations. Authoritarian governments, while very powerful, are obliged to acknowledge certain limits to their power that may be imposed by the economic elite and/or the

---

governing panels (which are probably not appointed by popular vote). Examples of countries with authoritarian governments include Saudi Arabia and Kuwait.

11.3.2 Totalitarian

A totalitarian government is one in which there are, in principle, no recognizable limits to authority that rulers are willing to acknowledge. In a totalitarian government, the power to make final decisions often rests in the hands of a single ruler and cannot be appealed. It relies on the military for full and unrelenting enforcement of its edicts. The government extends control over many aspects of citizens' lives.

11.3.3 Democratic

A democratic government is one in which authority ultimately lies with the people whose participation in government (i.e., both in the decision-making processes as well as in the process of appointing, electing, or dismissing rulers) is considered a right.

Problem Solving Example:

In the sense of the decision-making process, how is totalitarianism more efficient than democracy?

In totalitarian systems, every aspect of society is regulated by the government and its members. A small group controls the political process and, though voting may be allowed, opposition candidates are not permitted. Dissension is suppressed and culture is regulated to control nonconforming or threatening ideas and messages. Without opposition, decisions can be made unimpeded. By saving massive amounts of time and bureaucratic resources, the totalitarian system is more streamlined than democratic systems, where opposition and dissension are permitted and citizens are protected from abusive government.

11.4 The Political Process

A political party is an organization seeking to gain control of government through legitimate means. In the U.S., where many people hold political attitudes that are both liberal and conservative, party identification is relatively weak.

Interest groups are those groups or organizations seeking to influence political decisions that may affect their members. They are political alliances of people who are interested in some social or economic issue. Lobbyists are the advocates or the "voice" of special interest groups.

11.5 C. Wright Mills' *The Power Elite*

In 1956, C. Wright Mills published *The Power Elite*. Looking at the social class of leaders in major areas of influence and authority (including business and government), he found that they not only share a singular vision of what is fair and good, but also that they act in ways that serve their interest in maintaining the existing stratification system and, thereby, their position in it.

In Mills' terms, at the highest level of power are "warlords, corporate chieftains, and the political directorate," who together, and in cooperation with one another, comprise America's power elite. A highly organized group of only a few people who make decisions on behalf of the many, the power elite consists of military leaders, politicians, and business leaders who are responsible to no one but themselves.

11.6 G. William Domhoff's Governing Class

Attempting to learn whether or not America has the sort of ruling class described by Mills, G. William Domhoff studied the people listed in the Social Register to identify those who have attended select private schools, who are millionaires, and who are members of prestigious men's clubs in large cities. He found that these people, who comprise the upper class in America, represent less than 0.5 percent of the population.

Besides being extremely wealthy, many upper-class people hold high-level positions in corporations, banks, insurance companies, the CIA, government offices, the mass media, charitable organizations, and as trustees of colleges and universities. They also comprise a close-knit group of people united by intermarriage, through their educational experience of attending the same schools, as members of the same clubs, and as board members of the largest corporations.

11.7 David Riesman's Pluralist Vision

Although agreeing with Mills that there is an unequal distribution of power in the United States, David Riesman (1961) rejects the notion that the power holders are, or can be, a unified group. The diversity of interests that exists in mass society makes it impossible for any single group to dominate society by controlling the decision-making process. Thus, Riesman understood the system of rule to be made up of various sectors of power, each serving as a potential buffer against any one group gaining control of the decision-making process throughout the system.

Problem Solving Example:

Q Bob believes most modern societies are ruled by an elite group of powerful people who unite their resources and make decisions to secure their positions and maintain the status quo. Consider the research of Domhoff, Mills, and Riesman. How do they support or challenge Bob's contention?

A Domhoff's study of the Social Register would support the belief in a powerful elite. Domhoff found that the American upper class holds high-level positions in corporations, banks, insurance companies, government, and the mass media. Mills found that leaders in business and government share a vision and act to promote their positions and interests. Thus, Mills' findings would support Bob's beliefs. However, David Riesman has argued that society's system of rule contains various sectors of power, each serving as a potential buffer against any one group gaining excessive control of the decision-making process. The diversity of interests that exists in mass society makes it impossible for any single group to dominate society. Therefore, Riesman would not support Bob's belief.

Quiz: Politics and Society

1. Some parts of the political system in the United States utilize laws and bureaucratic rules to define who has what kind of power and authority over whom. These laws and rules exemplify which type of authority?

    (A) Traditional

    (B) Charismatic

    (C) Legal-rational

    (D) Institutionalized

    (E) Corporate

2. According to C. Wright Mills' concept of the power elite, most leaders in major areas of influence and authority are united in their agenda to

    (A) act in ways that maintain the existing stratification and their position in it.

    (B) control the means of production.

    (C) keep the lower state in conflict.

    (D) remind citizens of their individual roles in the over-all system.

    (E) All of the above.

3. The idea that we should continue to follow the norms and laws of society because that is what we have always done is an illustration of

    (A) legal-rational authority.

    (B)   traditional authority.

    (C)   charismatic authority.

    (D)   court precedent.

    (E)   a system of sanctions.

4.   All of the following characteristics are elements of a totalitarian government EXCEPT

    (A)   government control of the media.

    (B)   government control of the military.

    (C)   government control of the educational system.

    (D)   an ideology that legitimates the current state.

    (E)   several political parties.

5.   Lobbyists act as the voice of _____ seeking to influence political decisions that may affect them.

    (A)   political parties

    (B)   politicians

    (C)   interest groups

    (D)   dictators

    (E)   corporate chieftains

6.   What model of political institutions assumes that there are different bases of power that compete with each other?

    (A)   Power elite

    (B)   Democratic

    (C)   Pluralist

    (D)   Monopolistic

    (E)   None of the above.

7.   Saudi Arabia and Kuwait are examples of countries with governments in which rulers tolerate little opposition to their reigns. What name have sociologists given this type of government?

   (A)   Democracy

   (B)   Monarchy

   (C)   Republic

   (D)   Traditional

   (E)   Authoritarian

8.   In a(n) _____ government, authority lies with the people who have the right to participate in government by appointing, electing, or dismissing rulers.

   (A)   Western

   (B)   modern

   (C)   partisan

   (D)   democratic

   (E)   autocratic

9.   Domhoff's research found that members of the Social Register who had attended select private schools, who were millionaires, and who were members of prestigious men's clubs in larger cities comprised less than _____ percent of the population.

   (A)   0.05

   (B)   0.5

   (C)   5

   (D)   50

   (E)   None of the above.

10. The right of those in positions of power to command is funda-
    mental to all forms of authority. What is this right called?

    (A) Divine right

    (B) Charisma

    (C) Tradition

    (D) Socialism

    (E) Legitimacy

ANSWER KEY

1.	(C)		6.	(C)
2.	(A)		7.	(E)
3.	(B)		8.	(D)
4.	(E)		9.	(B)
5.	(C)		10.	(E)

CHAPTER 12

Society and Religion

12.1 Religion and Society

The term *religion* means a theory, creed, or body of dogma that seeks to comprehend the universe and man's place in it, God or the gods, and the supernatural realm overall. Every religion seeks to establish a meaningful, coherent image of the natural and supernatural worlds. For some sociologists, however, religion represents more than just a "system" or methodically organized set of beliefs. Religion constitutes a totality of commonly held beliefs and rites oriented toward the realm of the sacred or supernatural. In this sense, every religion is thought to be social in its origins and in its effects. Religion ultimately serves a cohesive function in maintaining the whole of society (See Durkheim, *The Elementary Forms of Religious Life*, 1912). Specifically, religions have been linked with:

1. Codes of ethics—This is the case with Confucianism—a very practical religion that places little emphasis on the supernatural world and a great deal of emphasis on seeing a situation for what it is, and then applying the rules that are appropriate to the situation.

2. Personality—Religion has been a factor in both the persecution or exaltation of certain groups, as well as the development of social mores. For these reasons, the religious climate

can have a dramatic effect on the personality of an individual or community.

3. Historical condition—Religion has also fostered polarized world-views that tend to have a "this-worldly" or an "other-worldly" orientation, such as medieval monasticism, which emphasized withdrawal from this world in order to prepare for eternity.

4. Theodicy—A religious explanation for what seems to be the senseless distribution of good and bad fortune that enables believers to maintain their faith under any circumstances.

12.2 The Sacred and the Profane

Sacred refers to the sphere of ideas, activities, persons, objects, abilities, and experiences that have been deemed holy, divine, supernatural, or mystical and, hence, unalterable. Profane refers to the visceral sphere of objects, persons, and behaviors capable of being understood and of being altered.

12.3 Durkheim

Emile Durkheim saw religion as validating the existence of society. In *The Elementary Forms of Religious Life*, Durkheim states that the collective experience of religious society serves not only as the foundation for ideas about life's ultimate meaning, but also for the ceremonies that seek to express this meaning.

12.4 Weber

Concerned about the relationship between thought and action, Max Weber studied the central tenets of Islam, Buddhism, Hinduism, Confucianism, Christianity, and Judaism to determine how each established psychological and practical grounds for economic activity. In *The Protestant Ethic and the Spirit of Capitalism*, Weber showed how Protestant belief in predestination and an unbridgeable gulf between man and God emphasized personal responsibility for one's own salvation. The measure of a person's success and blessing was illustrated by how much material wealth could be accumulated before death. The fact that God allowed one to accumulate so much wealth was ready proof that God approved of the selfless approach to that success. This generated an anxiety regarding one's status in the after-life that proved to be compatible with a work ethic that called for the accumulation of capital as indicative of salvation.

Problem Solving Example:

Q Anna has been studying the personal correspondence of mem-bers of a small religious community living in the Midwest in the 1930s. She has noticed the letters' references to hard work, personal responsibility, and thrift. How is Anna's work related to the classic work of Max Weber?

A In his book *The Protestant Ethic and the Spirit of Capital-ism*, Weber wrote that central to the Protestant belief in personal salvation is the idea of work as a "calling," as a holy obli-gation. It follows, according to Weber, that working hard at a holy obligation reaps rewards, so success is a sign of God's favor. Weber found that the Protestant belief in personal salvation led to anxiety about the afterlife, which was compatible with a work ethic that viewed accumulation of capital as proof of salvation. Additionally, the early Protestants, who rejected ostentatious displays of wealth, tended to invest their earnings. These practices appear to parallel Anna's findings.

12.5 Forms of Religious Organization—Cult, Sect, Church

The simplest form of religious organization, a cult, consists of a small group of followers surrounding a charismatic religious leader. A sect, unlike a cult, does not depend on the kind of personal inspiration offered by a charismatic leader for its continuity. A sect is a religious denomination derived, but deviating from, a readily accepted tradition. Typically, a church claims universal membership over those born into it, and they can only leave it through expulsion. This is the very opposite of a cult in that its leadership is formally established, its economic foundation has been institutionalized, membership is by birth (not voluntary), and sanctions take the form of interdiction and excommunication.

Problem Solving Example:

Q Kate has an interest in the evolution of religious practice in a small southern community. During her interviews with residents of the community, she has noted several references to a group about which she has been unable to locate any information. She does not believe it is an established religious institution, but she is not sure it is a cult. What criterion should Kate use to categorize this form of religious organization?

A A cult consists of a small group of followers surrounding a charismatic leader. Sects do not depend on the personal inspiration of a leader, and churches are formally established institutions that sanction their members. Thus, Kate should note characteristics, such as the size of the group, its leadership, and its practices of recruiting members.

12.6 World Religions

World religion is understood as "a system of life regulation" capable of attracting a multitude of constituents. Thus, the religious ethics of the Confucian, Hindu, Buddhist, Christian, and Muslim faiths belong to what Max Weber characterized as "the category of world religions."

Unlike those religions of the West and Middle East—Judaism, Christianity, and Islam—which emphasize one God (monotheism) and "this-worldliness," the religions of Southeast Asia and the Far East not only tend to be oriented toward nature and the afterlife, but also tend to be polytheistic (emphasizing many gods). Buddhism, Hinduism, Shintoism, and Confucianism address questions relating to humanity's place in the universe, the path to happiness, and the meaning of life. Thus, unlike Islam, Judaism, and Christianity, which stress the importance of received doctrine, these other religions stress the element of soul searching and other techniques for solving the riddle of life's ultimate meaning.

Quiz: Society and Religion

1. That religion serves to unite people into a single moral community most closely describes the viewpoint of

    (A)   Emile Durkheim.

    (B)   Karl Marx.

    (C)   Max Weber.

    (D)   Herbert Spencer.

    (E)   George Herbert Mead.

2. The German sociologist Max Weber is best known for his study

    (A)   *Street Corner Society.*

    (B)   *The Division of Labor in Society.*

    (C)   *The Human Group.*

    (D)   *The Protestant Ethic and the Spirit of Capitalism.*

    (E)   *The Theory of the Leisure Class.*

3. What is the name sociologists have given to the sphere of ideas, activities, persons, objects, abilities, and experiences that have been deemed holy, divine or supernatural, and unalterable?

    (A)   Scripture

    (B)   Sacred

    (C)   Holy orders

    (D)   Charisma

    (E)   Rites

4. In comparison to a cult, a _____ has formally established leadership, is an institutionalized economic foundation, confers membership to those born into it, and sanctions members through interdiction or excommunication.

    (A) church

    (B) sect

    (C) religion

    (D) community

    (E) colony

5. Unlike religions of the West and Middle East that emphasize one god, those of Southeast Asia and the Far East tend to be

    (A) atheistic.

    (B) agnostic.

    (C) polytheistic.

    (D) monotheistic.

    (E) Protestant.

6. A term which explains a believer's ability to hold on to faith in spite of the random distribution of good and bad fortune is

    (A) therapeutic.

    (B) theodicy.

    (C) theology.

    (D) thematic.

    (E) None of the above.

7. A theory, creed, or body of dogma that seeks to comprehend the universe and man's place in it is called a

    (A) social system.

    (B) social order.

    (C) social rite.

    (D)   religion.

    (E)   folkway.

8.   Confucianism places little emphasis on the supernatural world; rather it promotes the application of rules to various situations. Sociologists refer to this system as a

    (A)   code of ethics.

    (B)   value system.

    (C)   moral compass.

    (D)   sacred text.

    (E)   None of the above.

9.   A _____ is a small group following a charismatic religious leader, while a _____ does not depend on the presence of a charismatic leader.

    (A)   colony, commune

    (B)   commune, colony

    (C)   cult, sect

    (D)   cult, commune

    (E)   sect, commune

10.   The sphere of objects, persons, and behaviors capable of being understood and altered is labeled in sociological terms as

    (A)   temporal.

    (B)   earthly.

    (C)   practical.

    (D)   profane.

    (E)   None of the above.

ANSWER KEY

1.	(A)	6.	(B)
2.	(D)	7.	(D)
3.	(B)	8.	(A)
4.	(A)	9.	(C)
5.	(C)	10.	(D)

CHAPTER 13

Defining Social Stratification

13.1 Social Stratification

Sociologists agree that societies are stratified, or arranged, along many levels. Where they begin to differ is on the question of what, if anything, the layers represent beyond the distinctions made among differing degrees of power, wealth, and social prestige.

Stratification and inequality are consistent with an orientation toward society; it is claimed that all societies make distinctions between people. There are some distinctions that always receive differential treatment—as between old and young, or male and female. There are other distinctions that may or may not receive differential treatment depending upon a given society's values. The usual result of a society treating people differently on the basis of their age, sex, race, religion, sexual orientation, or education is social inequality. This inequality can take the form of an unfair distribution of wealth, prestige, or power.

Social stratification, then, represents the structured inequality characterized by groups of people with differential access to the rewards of society because of their relative positions in the social hierarchy. Thus, a fundamental task of sociology is the determination of why stratified societies are so prevalent. With almost the entire human population living in such societies, sociologists must try to decide whether stratification is inevitable and, if so, the effects of social inequality.

13.2 Life Chances

Sociologists have found that those in the same social stratum generally share the same life chances or opportunities. They seem to benefit or suffer equally from whatever advantages or disadvantages society has to offer.

13.3 Stratification and Social Structure

Consistent with an orientation toward social structure, stratification systems serve to rank some people (whether individuals or groups) as more deserving of power, wealth, and prestige than others.

13.3.1 Social Hierarchy

The inevitable result of this stratification is a social hierarchy of ranked statuses in which people function. These statuses may be either ascribed or achieved. An ascribed social position is either received at birth, or involuntarily placed upon an individual later in life. An achieved social position is usually assumed voluntarily and generally reflects personal ability or effort. Individuals in a society are treated differently depending on where their social positions stand in the overall social hierarchy.

13.3.2 Social Mobility

Social mobility refers to the ability of a given individual or group to move through the social strata. Structural mobility refers to factors at the societal level that affect mobility rates. For example, the numbers and types of available jobs, dependent on changes in the economic system, have a profound effect on social mobility. In addition, the number of people available to fill those jobs will fluctuate depending on the birthrates of both current and previous generations.

Social mobility may be either relative or absolute. An example of relative mobility would be the upgrade of an entire occupational structure, such that only the content of the work changes, not its relative position in the social hierarchy from one generation to the next. An example of absolute mobility would be when a son's education, occupational prestige, and income exceed those of his father.

Problem Solving Example:

Q Walter was born on a small farm in rural Kansas. Walter's father did not finish high school. Walter, however, did. He received a scholarship to college, from which he graduated with honors. How would a sociologist measure Walter's absolute social mobility?

A Social mobility refers to the ability of a person or group to move through social strata, often measured by educational attainment, occupational prestige, and income. Absolute mobility for Walter would be measured by his education, occupational prestige, and income exceeding that of his father. His social mobility improved when he finished high school and again when he finished college with honors. Further mobility will depend on his career choices and subsequent economic returns.

13.4 Systems of Stratification

A system of stratification refers to the institutions and ideas that permit or limit the distribution of prestige, status, and opportunities in life. Based on the degree of significance attached to certain values in a particular society at a particular time, and the extent to which a particular group monopolizes the areas in which the values are available as evidenced by the development or decline of institutions, stratification may have several sources. These sources—which include race, ethnicity, gender, age, and sexual orientation—at times have served as the basis for assigning inferior or superior status to entire populations.

13.4.1 Race and Ethnicity

Sociologists consider race to be as much, if not more, of a cultural phenomenon than a biological one. In biological terms, a person's race tends to be identified by a range of genetically determined characteristics, such as skin and hair color, facial features, and body type. These variations in population were once easily associated with geography—certain physical traits became associated with people living in specific areas of the world. However, the human population is now far more mobile, and intermarriage between groups that were once geographically isolated from one another is now commonplace. That we categorize people into "races" is a social phenomenon rather than a biological one. In fact, a discussion of race in biological terms serves no useful purpose. Society, not biology, categorizes people into races.

Ethnicity refers to a population known and identified on the basis of its common language, national heritage, and/or biological inheritance. While race primarily refers to differences in physical characteristics, ethnic differences are culturally learned and not genetically inherited.

Problem Solving Example:

Q Bert is interested in studying race as a source for social stratification. To prepare for his study, he is consulting biology texts to create definitions and categories for various racial groups. What is the greatest challenge to Bert's research?

A Because sociologists consider race a social phenomenon, the biologists' definition would be meaningless for sociological inquiry. Society, not biology, categorizes people into races. Additionally, if Bert were to employ a biological perspective in his research, he would find that pure races don't exist. However, a related term, ethnicity, refers to a population known and identified on the basis of common language, heritage, and/or biological inheritance and is useful to sociologists. In his study, Bert would be wise to use those racial categories developed by demographers (social scientists who study the characteristics of human populations), understanding that these categories are fundamentally arbitrary and prone to change over time.

13.4.2 Gender

Gender stratification refers to those different roles and positions assigned to males and females in a society based on differences between men and women that have been acquired or learned. Gender is defined as the social behavior that is deemed to be appropriate to 'masculine' or 'feminine' roles and learned through primary and secondary socialization. It encompasses differences in hairstyles, types and styles of clothing worn, and in family and occupational roles. Across societies, women have been systematically denied certain rights and opportunities based on assumptions regarding their abilities. This inferior status of women has often been legitimized through a sexist ideology (a belief system assuming that inborn/innate characteristics translate into one gender being superior to another) which is passed on across generations via culture.

13.4.3 Age

Age stratification refers to the ways in which people are treated differentially depending on their age. This form of stratification is reflective of the attitudes and behaviors we associate with age, and of the different roles and statuses we assign to people depending upon their ages.

13.4.4 Sexual Orientation

Stratification on the basis of sexual orientation or affection refers to the ways in which individuals are differentially treated on the basis of their sexual preferences. In some societies, the results of this stratification are relatively benign; however, in other societies, results of this stratification have also taken the form of criminalization of same-sex unions, as well as discrimination in housing, employment, and social status. Many societies forbid homosexual marriages, thereby systematically excluding homosexual couples from the social and economic benefits of marriage. In addition, this exclusion from major social institutions has often translated into a perceived social acceptance of discrimination against homosexuals.

13.5 Davis and Moore—A Functionalist View of Social Stratification

In their classic presentation of the functionalist view of stratification, Kingsley Davis and Wilbert Moore (1945) argue that some stratification is necessary. Not everyone has the same abilities. At any given time, some members of a society will have more of the qualities that are needed and desired than others. Also, some roles will be more essential to the effective functioning of the society than others. Thus, in order to attract people with the requisite talents and skills to these more demanding, often stressful, roles, which also involve prolonged training and sacrifice, a society must offer greater rewards and higher status. In this way, inequality (the unequal distribution of social rewards) is considered functional for society in that it guarantees that those most able will be in the most demanding positions. Social stratification, in other words, is inevitable.

13.6 Marx, Weber, and Modern Conflict Theory

Marx attributed inequalities of wealth, power, and prestige to the economic situation that class structures present. Thus, the elimination of classes would serve to put an end to inequality, to the exploitation of man by man, and to the basic conflict of interest between the haves and the have nots. According to Marx, the elimination of class structure would also enable men and women to regain their humanity through the creation of a genuine or true community "where individuals gain their freedom in and through their association" (See Marx, *The Poverty of Philosophy*, 1963).

By contrast, Weber distinguished between class, status situation, and parties as a step toward explaining the origins of the different economic, social, political, and religious situations of society that he saw in India, China, ancient Greece, Rome, and the West (extending from Great Britain to Russia). By class, he meant economic situation as defined by wealth, property, and other opportunities for income. A status situation consisted of every aspect of a person's life linked to the positive or negative characterization of that status. Parties were groups oriented toward acquiring social power (i.e., opportunities to realize their common goals despite resistance).

Focused on the origins of man-made culture, Weber often found such differences to be a source of conflict and change that he could not foresee ending. He discovered various systems of stratification. Some modes of organization were based on caste, where social mobility is not permitted by religious sanctions. Others were based on class, including the feudal system of medieval society that was based on vassalage, or reciprocal obligations of loyalty and service between lord and knight, or lord and serf.

Modern conflict theory continues to struggle with the question of the basis of conflict. Believing that Marx placed too much emphasis on class, Ralf Dahrendorf (1959) focused on the struggle among groups, such as unions and employers. Randall Collins continued to focus on the way that different groups seek to maintain their social positions by acquiring educational credentials that they then use to secure jobs and other advantages. Still others see the conflict over ideological hegemony, including beliefs, attitudes, and ideals, as being the decisive element distinguishing the higher from the lower strata.

Problem Solving Example:

Q What is the most significant difference between Karl Marx and Max Weber regarding conflict theory?

A Marx and Weber approached their studies of conflict from different perspectives. Marx held that the unequal distribution of wealth, power, prestige, and the conflicts associated with them were caused by economic systems of the industrial period. On the other hand, Weber contended that culture (especially religion) shaped human action—economic, social, political, and religious situations. Marx held that conflict would be eliminated only when social classes were eliminated, but Weber could foresee no ending to conflict. In short, Marx believed that class arose from economic systems. Weber believed that class was a factor in the creation of economic (and political, social, and religious) systems.

Quiz: Defining Social Stratification

1. When sociologists use the term "ethnic group", they are referring to people who have

    (A)   a shared cultural heritage.

    (B)   low social status.

    (C)   similar physical appearance.

    (D)   common political views.

    (E)   the same occupation.

2.   As defined by Weber, _____ are groups oriented toward gaining social power.

    (A)   governments

    (B)   bureaucracies

    (C)   organizations

    (D)   parties

    (E)   All of the above.

3.   The division of society into status positions is called

    (A)   stratification.

    (B)   social mobility.

    (C)   status inconsistency.

    (D)   the power elite.

    (E)   social evaluation.

4.   Marx attributed the inequalities of wealth, power, and prestige to

    (A)   culture.

    (B)   communism.

    (C)   colonialism.

    (D)   class.

    (E)   charisma.

5.   According to the functionalist theory of stratification developed by Kingsley Davis and Wilbert Moore, some occupations are more highly rewarded than others because they

    (A)   have been held for a long time.

    (B)   are organized into unions.

(C)   require physical labor.

(D)   appeal to widely shared values.

(E)   require long periods of training.

6.   Many societies forbid homosexual marriages; this excludes homosexual couples from the _____ benefits of marriage.

(A)   primary and secondary

(B)   racial and ethnic

(C)   social and economic

(D)   emotional and psychological

(E)   None of the above.

7.   With respect to gender roles, most sociologists would argue that gender role differences are largely a result of

(A)   biology.

(B)   individual psychology.

(C)   socialization.

(D)   the Oedipus complex.

(E)   sociobiology.

8.   Members of the same social stratum generally share the same benefits or suffer equally from whatever advantages or disadvantages society has to offer. Sociologists refer to these circumstances and outcomes as

(A)   social status.

(B)   social order.

(C)   bias.

(D)   stratification.

(E)   life chances.

9. Social mobility refers to

    (A) gaining a college education.

    (B) entering any occupation one chooses.

    (C) traveling freely across national borders.

    (D) changing one's social class position.

    (E) marrying a person of another religion.

10. Unlike Marx, Weber did not define class in terms of relationship to the means of production. Rather, Weber defined class in terms of _____ situations as defined by wealth, property, and other opportunities for income.

    (A) social

    (B) political

    (C) cultural

    (D) psychological

    (E) economic

ANSWER KEY

1.	(A)	6.	(C)
2.	(D)	7.	(C)
3.	(A)	8.	(E)
4.	(D)	9.	(D)
5.	(E)	10.	(E)

CHAPTER 14

Collective Behavior, Social Movements, and Social Change

14.1 Defining Collective Behavior

Collective behavior means group behavior that, though rarely random, generally occurs in the absence of clearly defined and conventional norms. Such behavior may arise spontaneously and is less stable than institutionalized forms of collective behavior. As such, collective behavior generally lacks institutional backing and represents a collective response to changed cultural or social circumstances. Whether sporadic and short-lived, or relatively continuous and longer-lasting, collective behavior can be hard to predict because it does not arise in response to cultural or social norms. For this reason, it is even more difficult to observe or measure objectively because it is always in a continual state of flux.

14.2 Relatively Spontaneous Expressions of Collective Behavior

Collective behavior, which is relatively spontaneous, includes both short-lived, spontaneous public expressions of feeling without clear-cut goals and longer-lasting public expressions that are aimed at being instrumental in achieving clear-cut goals. Such behavior includes mass hysteria, panics, crazes, fads, fashions, and rumors.

14.2.1 Mass Hysteria

Mass hysteria represents a collective emotional response to tension and anxiety in a group. Such a response cannot be controlled and involves deep-seated emotions on the part of group members who, feeling deprived or powerless, may be responding to such feelings.

14.2.2 Panic

A panic, in the sense that sociologists use the term, is a collective action caused by the overwhelming feeling and awareness of needing to escape a dangerous situation immediately. For example, when a fire breaks out in a movie theater, few social norms exist that specify the appropriate action to take. The result may be people panicking and trampling one another in an attempt to escape.

14.2.3 Craze

A craze is a situation of collective behavior in which people become obsessed with wanting something because of the popular belief that "everyone else" seems to have it.

14.2.4 Fad

A fad represents the type of short-term obsession with a behavior that is unexpected and widely copied, like streaking.

14.2.5 Fashion

Unlike the obsessions with mannerisms, objects, and speech that crazes and fads represent, fashions are more widely held beliefs, styles, and attitudes toward dress, hairstyles, music, etc. They usually spread throughout the general population and last longer.

14.2.6 Rumor

A rumor is a piece of unconfirmed public information that may or may not be accurate. Typically, the source of the rumor is anonymous.

Problem Solving Example:

Q Helen has been researching the behavior of her classmates at a small college in New England. She has been documenting her classmates' clothing, hairstyle, and musical preferences. Here are some notes from Helen's journal: "Spring 2012, sandals and heavy, brightly colored cotton socks are popular with men and women; Fall 2012, many women shave heads to show solidarity for women in the military; Spring 2013, concerts by nationally known feminist musicians are sold out." Identify each of the behaviors from Helen's journal as fads, crazes, or fashions.

A Sociologists define fads as short-term obsessions with behavior that is unexpected. The shaved heads are a fad. Crazes are obsessions with wanting something because "everyone else" seems to have it. The sandals and socks are a craze. Fashions are long-lasting, widespread, and generally socially important. The popularity of feminist musicians is most likely a fashion.

14.3 Other Forms of Collective Behavior— Crowds

A crowd is a relatively large number of people in close proximity to one another, reacting at once to a common interest or focus. Some examples of crowds include spectators at a football game, participants at a parade, and rioters. There is milling on the part of crowd participants, whose physical movements not only express restlessness and excitement, but also are the basis for communication that results in the situation becoming collectively defined and action becoming collectively initiated. As members of an anonymous crowd, people tend to be open to suggestion and to feel a sense of urgency. However, crowds are not completely void of structure. Even when rioting, participants conform to specific patterns of behavior.

14.3.1 Masses

A mass refers to those people who are similarly concerned with the same problems or phenomena without necessarily being together in the same place at the same time.

14.3.2 Audiences, Mobs and Riots

An audience is a type of "passive crowd" that is both oriented toward and responding to a social situation (concert, lecture, sporting event, religious service, burning building) in a relatively orderly and predictable way. A mob is a type of crowd that is easily aroused and easily bent to taking aggressive action of a violent or disruptive nature. A riot, generally speaking, is not as spontaneous as a mob action, even though riots tend to involve larger numbers of people and usually last longer.

Problem Solving Example:

Q Radi has been studying the behavior of young concertgoers and has noticed what she believes is a merging of audience (what some have called conventional crowd) and mob behaviors. She has noticed wild dancing in areas near the stage and incidents of audience members jumping onto dancing crowd members from the stage. Radi is attempting to mark when an audience, or passive crowd, becomes a mob. For what kinds of behavior should Radi be looking?

A Though both audiences and mobs feature people milling about in close proximity, a conventional crowd is relatively orderly. Audiences respond in fairly predictable ways—clapping, whistling, and waving their hands about. A mob, on the other hand, is bent more toward aggressive action to effect some change. What Radi is most likely seeing is behavior midway between a conventional crowd and a mob—in other words, an expressive crowd in which audience responses go beyond the controlling norms of conventional crowds, but are not directed at achieving some change.

14.4 Other Aspects of Collective Behavior— Public Versus Private

The public represents those people in a population with a general interest in, and opinion about, an issue of concern to them. Public opinion refers to the actual opinions people have about a given issue. Propaganda refers to those attempts to affect and change what the public sees and how the public perceives an issue.

14.5 Explaining Collective Behavior

Social scientists have attempted to make sense of unconventional collective behavior over the last century. Contagion, convergence, and emergent-norm theories have been most successful in achieving that end.

14.5.1 Contagion Theory

Contagion theory, developed by Gustave Le Bon (1896), contends that crowds create a distinct milieu that powerfully influences its members. A crowd, made up of numerous anonymous individuals, frees its members from personal responsibility and social restraints. The individual members then succumb to the collective mind of the crowd.

14.5.2 Convergence Theory

Convergence theory posits that the individuals, not the crowd, possess particular motivations. When a number of like-minded individuals converge, they are likely to generate a collective action. For example, rioters in Los Angeles may have all been reacting to feelings of oppression and racism, as embodied by the acquittal of police officers accused of beating black motorist Rodney King. The rioters emerged from a convergence of people sharing a desire for racial equality.

14.5.3 Emergent-Norm Theory

Emergent-norm theory, developed by Ralph Turner and Lewis Killian (1987), argues that crowds do not necessarily begin with individuals sharing the same interests and motives. Instead, certain individuals construct new norms, which are soon adopted by the entire collective. An example is when an individual throws a rock at a policeman and a number of others follow suit. Others may follow shortly after because a new set of expected behaviors (norms) has been created.

Problem Solving Example:

Q Betty has been studying collective behavior in the context of urban riots. She is searching for a theory that best represents her idea that a rioting crowd has a mind of its own. Describe three theories of collective behavior and how they support or refute Betty's theory.

A Gustave Le Bon's contagion theory contends that a crowd exerts a powerful influence over its members. Crowds consist of anonymous individuals who are free of personal responsibility and restraint. This allows the individual to succumb to the collective mind of the crowd. Le Bon's theory would support Betty's contention. Convergence theory, on the other hand, holds that individuals meet other like-minded individuals in crowds where they generate collective action. In effect, the crowd is simply the merging of individual, yet cooperative, wills. This theory would not support Betty's idea. In emergent-norm theory, Turner and Killian argued that crowds are moved by the norms introduced by certain individuals. This theory would support Betty's contention that the urban riot represents a single will, though the will develops as new norms are identified and embraced.

14.6 Social Movements

A social movement is constituted by a set of beliefs, opinions, interests, and practices generally favoring institutional change of a particular or more general sort. In this context, a countermovement exists when members of a population have opinions and beliefs that they act on in a way which shows their opposition to a particular movement. Institutionalization is the process whereby the ideas of those involved in a social movement come to be known and accepted, serving as the foundation of social organization. Goal displacement occurs when the original goals of a movement are rejected or set aside in favor of the goal of preserving formal structures.

Social movement organizations are those formal organizations that are specifically created for the purpose of channeling either dissatisfaction and discontent into change, or satisfaction and contentment into conservation of tradition. This occurs both at the public level of government policy and at the private level of concrete action.

Problem Solving Example:

Q Maria is studying the growth of feminism among Catholic Hispanic women in a small community in the Southwest. Among her observations, Maria has found that only five percent of the women are employed outside of the home, and none of them have education beyond the 10th grade. None of them reported having voted in the two most recent general elections, though 85 percent of their husbands did. None of them reported practicing contraception, and 96 percent reported that an unmarried woman should live with her parents until she is wed. From her observations, Maria has hypothesized that feminism has failed to develop as a social movement among this group of women. What in her findings supports Maria's hypothesis?

A Social movements are constituted by a set of beliefs, opinions, interests, and practices that generally favor institutional change. Maria's findings show that the Catholic Hispanic women in her study failed to embrace feminist beliefs and practices that favored institutional change. Instead, her findings indicate that few of the women have ventured beyond traditional sex roles in this community—working almost exclusively in the home—as opposed to attaining higher education that might lead to other occupational opportunities. None have displayed interest in civic activity—such as voting, which is a major tenet of the feminist movement. And the majority of her subjects appear to believe that unmarried women are subordinate to their parents until they are married, after which they are subordinate to their husbands. Of course, Maria would have to conduct further study to eliminate other possible reasons for these observations, such as economic deprivation or the concept of "homemaker" as an occupation which is valuable and marketable.

Quiz: Collective Behavior, Social Movements, and Social Change

1. An organized effort to promote some form of social change is called

    (A) collective behavior.

    (B) mob behavior.

    (C) a riot.

    (D) a social movement.

    (E) a crowd.

2. A widespread desire to own toys and dolls based on a particular television show is an example of a

    (A) social movement.

    (B) fashion.

    (C) mob.

    (D) fad.

    (E) None of the above.

3. Sociologists refer to anonymous, unconfirmed information as

    (A) constructive.

    (B) destructive.

    (C) unending.

    (D) powerful.

    (E) rumor.

4. When an individual throws a rock at a police officer and several others follow suit, a new set of expected behaviors may have been created. This is an illustration of the _____ theory of collective behavior.

    (A) inner-city

    (B) public-protest

    (C) passive resistance

    (D) emergent-norm

    (E) None of the above.

5. Similar concerns about a problem or phenomenon appeal to _____ of individuals though they are not together at the same place or time.

    (A) masses

    (B) mobs

    (C) mentors

    (D) members

    (E) None of the above.

6. In _____ theory, a number of like-minded individuals come together to generate collective action.

    (A) conspiracy

    (B) convergence

    (C) conflict

    (D) compromise

    (E) None of the above.

7. A passive crowd that responds to a social situation in an orderly, predictable way is

    (A) a crowd.

    (B) a mob.

   (C)   a community.

   (D)   an audience.

   (E)   a group of fans.

8.   Though not as spontaneous as mobs, _____ are larger and usually last longer.

   (A)   fads

   (B)   crazes

   (C)   crowds

   (D)   riots

   (E)   None of the above.

9.   The people in a population with a general interest in, and who have an opinion about, an issue are described as the

   (A)   electorate.

   (B)   government.

   (C)   public.

   (D)   taxpayers.

   (E)   None of the above.

10.   An individual succumbing to the collective mind of a crowd is an example of the _____ theory, first developed by Gustave Le Bon.

   (A)   crowd

   (B)   conflict

   (C)   conspiracy

   (D)   conservative

   (E)   contagion

ANSWER KEY

1.	(D)	6.	(B)
2.	(D)	7.	(D)
3.	(E)	8.	(D)
4.	(D)	9.	(C)
5.	(A)	10.	(E)

NOTES

NOTES

NOTES

NOTES

NOTES

NOTES

NOTES

NOTES

NOTES

NOTES

NOTES